Post-Covid Future Exposed!

The great reset, build back better and total economic collapse

-

Agenda 2021 - 2030 – population Control – globalist future?

Rebel Press Media

Disclaimer

Our other books

Check out our other books for other unreported news, exposed facts and debunked truths, and more.

Join the exclusive Rebel Press Media Circle!

You will get new updates about the unreported reality delivered in your inbox every Friday.

Sign up here today:

https://campsite.bio/rebelpressmedia

Introduction

"The Authority seeks to procure a framework agreement for temporary body storage in the event of an excess deaths situation for the 32 London boroughs and the City of London, led by Westminster City Council. The framework agreement will appoint a single provider and will be for a period of 4 years. This will be a contingency contract, only called upon in the event that an excess deaths situation arises in the future and existing local body storage capacity needs to be augmented."

The UK government issued a tender on June 10 for 'temporary body storage facilities' in the London area in case there is going to be an 'excess number of deaths' over the next 6 months to 4 years. Many people now realize that if this is indeed going to happen, although these deaths will be attributed to the Delta variant or another Covid mutation, in reality they will most likely be vaccine victims.

A reader we spoke to recently made the comparison to the run-up to World War II, when Winston Churchill, in preparation for the war (otherwise shown to have been planned by both sides), ordered mass graves to be dug "in case" London was bombed. Hundreds of British citizens who wanted to publish or criticize evidence of the war conspiracy were arrested and imprisoned by Churchill without trial. Is history going to repeat itself, only this time with mass vaccinations and its opponents?

3

Looking ahead in 2020

In November 2020, the British government was already "urgently seeking an Artificial Intelligence (AI) program to handle the expected high number of serious adverse reactions (ADRs) to the Covid-19 vaccine. ADRs, Adverse Drug Reactions, we had translated with 'serious adverse reactions', because this does not mean ordinary side effects. ADRs include deaths, life-threatening diseases and permanent disabilities. Therefore, an ADR always requires hospitalization.

Vaccinations, which contain ingredients (mRNA / genetic instructions to make the most dangerous protein of the coronavirus in your own body) that you can NEVER get out of your body, do exactly what is strictly forbidden for food and drink. Worse still: the government is exerting ever-increasing pressure on the population to take JUST that vaccine, of which, again (we cannot emphasize it often enough), it is already known that it will cause a high number of casualties, including deaths.'

'What do you call a government that knowingly, deliberately and actively endangers the welfare of its own people, that deliberately forces something on its own population that it already knows in advance is going to cause a large number of sick and dead?'

Cynically, we could call that a government with a particularly 'far-sighted' approach. Like now in England, where they want to make room in advance for an obviously expected high number of corpses, caused by... what?

This book is a compilation of our articles published earlier and new articles to expose the vaccines with the fitting context, regarding topics such as depopulation and world control by the globalist elite, if you would like to know more about subjects such as the great reset, we would advice you to read our other books too, and share them with everyone you hold dear.

We want to reach as many people as possible, that's why keep publishing our content, to make sure that if one title gets ignored, the other title still gets the attention, these subjects need.

If we want to win this war against humanity, we have to inform everyone about the reality of what is happening right now!

Table of Contents

Chapter 1: August 2021?!

9.5% of fully vaccinated older people are still "not protected from dying," according to the UK government.

An official UK government document (dated March 31) on the 'Roadmap' as it is expected to be in 2021 shows that fully vaccinated seniors in particular should be concerned about the expected 'third corona wave' (which may or may not coincide with the Indian 'Delta' variant). On page 18, under item 56, there is something noteworthy, a disturbing statement that seems to confirm the likely scenario as we have been outlining it since spring 2020.

'This shows that most deaths and (hospital) admissions in a post-Roadmap resurgence (of corona (with a peak in August)) are people who received two vaccine doses, even without waning vaccine protection or an emerging variant escaping vaccines. This is because vaccine administration is so high in the highest age groups. Therefore, there are 5% of those over 50 who are not vaccinated, and 95% x 10% = 9.5% of those over 50 who are vaccinated but nevertheless not protected from mortality. This is not the result of ineffective vaccines, but only because vaccine administration is so high.' (emphasis added)

The 10% is the assumed seasonal variation in (virus) transmission. This seasonal variation, caused by 'the interplay between vaccination and infection-induced immunity', is expected to make the third wave (much) lower than the previous one, but may prolong the (assumed) 'epidemic'. It is also assumed that 90% of the population will be vaccinated until 50.

But please re-read this sentence again: *'This is not due to ineffective vaccines, but only because administration is so high.'*

The vaccines are "effective," but because we administer so many of them, 9.5% of those vaccinated over 50 are still not protected from death (by the coronavirus, not including mutations). What the government is saying with this tenebrous reasoning is that "just because we vaccinate so many people, statistically more vaccinated people will die.

But wait a minute, we vaccinate ALL those people to protect them from mortality, right? Then that vaccine should work on ALL those people, right? Perhaps you can maintain that the vaccine does not work in 0.1% or 1%, but in almost 10%? Compare that to the established Covid-19 IFR of only 0.15%. IF you get infected at all, you only have a 0.15% chance of dying from it (similar to seasonal flu). So why on earth would you take the risk of being injected with highly controversial experimental gene manipulation 'therapy'?

Broad vaccination during a pandemic was the stupidest thing you could do until 2020

9

If you were in favor of vaccinations at all then, perhaps the decision should be made to return to what was the general rule of thumb until 2020, namely that you only vaccinate high-risk groups? Numerous world-renowned top virologists and immunologists, including HIV discoverer and Nobel laureate Luc Montagnier, have warned on the basis of history that broadly vaccinating the entire (including healthy) population during an epidemic or pandemic - exactly what has been done everywhere since late last year - is the most stupid and harmful thing you can do.

'The models used here assume that the effectiveness of vaccines remains high, and do not consider the impact of new variants to be a cause for concern' (para. 61). Then, in point 63, this is already contradicted. 'The slow import of new variants, such as B.1.351., are a very important priority to develop the next generation of vaccines.' Since this will take 'many months', 'measures to prevent and manage import risk, such as testing of individuals... and maintaining strict quarantine measures for those entering the country remain important...'

Another piece of evidence to 100% mandatory vaccinations?

Is this document perhaps a disguised warning that 9.5% of the fully vaccinated elderly are 'not protected from mortality' precisely because of the vaccine? Is this trying to explain away in advance an expected very high number of vaccine deaths? Is this perhaps the real reason why the UK government is looking for sites to store an 'excess number of deaths' in London over the next 6 months to 4 years? 9.5% of 95% of 26 million British over-50s = 24.7 million = 2.35 million elderly people who could still die despite their vaccinations.

It's not explicitly written, but this premise does pave another piece of the way to the dreaded scenario of trying to enforce 100% mandatory vaccinations, and falsely blaming the few percent unvaccinated for this coming wave of illness and death, and the waves to come after that which are already being announced.

We can already guess the false propaganda messages of the system politicians and media: 'Only if everybody is vaccinated can this third wave/variant be stopped, your grandparents will be safe again, we won't have to announce new lockdowns,' et cetera. It will be repeated so often that the 90% who have made no effort whatsoever in the past eighteen months to do any critical research themselves, will blindly believe this umpteenth stream of demonstrable nonsense.

In any case, the British government is working ever more openly toward that goal: 'It is highly likely that new vaccines will be required in the medium term' (para. 64). 'If the epidemic grows larger as it did in the early autumn of 2020, then it is possible to have a controlled national scenario,' alongside possible regional and local measures.

Fake memorandum predicts permanent lockdown in a few weeks

A so-called British government memorandum would indicate that the country will go into permanent lockdown as early as 3 weeks or in August because - despite mass vaccinations - a 'third wave' with mainly the Indian Delta variant is expected. The document, whose authenticity cannot be confirmed and which is most likely fake*, is said to have been written by the infamous alarmist Dr. Neil M. Ferguson, who was discredited for his completely debunked pandemic models of last year, in which he predicted at least half a million deaths in Great Britain alone.

Chapter 2: Dump the vaccines?

"Norwegian government: Stopping this vaccine saves lives - EMA warns: AZ vaccine can also cause leaky blood vessels and very low blood pressure, with worst case kidney failure and brain hemorrhage"

Norway has decided to dump its stock of AstraZeneca vaccines in neighboring countries because you are statistically more likely to die from this vaccine than from Covid-19.

The FHI, Norway's version of the WHO, came to the decision because the AZ vaccine has been shown to cause serious complications such as blood clots, bleeding, and too low a platelet count. Dumping the vaccine now could save 10 people who would otherwise have died from the side effects. The AZ vaccine has a mortality rate of 2.3 in 100,000 in Norway, according to the FHI.

The authority is also against voluntary provision of the AZ vaccine, as it is considered 'unethical' to inject people with it 'who are not fully aware of the risk to which they are exposed'. Nevertheless, the supply is given to neighboring countries (along the lines of 'all lives are equal, but Norwegian lives are more equal than Swedish'?).

82% of Norwegians initially thought Covid vaccines were a good idea, but 76% are now skeptical. 99% do not want to be injected with AstraZeneca anyway; against the gene manipulation 'vaccines' of Moderna (9%) and Pfizer (8%) there is (still) much less distrust.

German scientists have discovered that the Johnson & Johnson vaccine carries the same risk of blood clots as the AstraZeneca vaccine. Meanwhile, the EMA warns of yet another potential side effect of the AZ vaccine: Capillary Leak Syndrome, which causes leaking blood vessels and very low blood pressure. This can lead to pain, nausea, fatigue, and in the worst case, kidney failure and brain hemorrhage.

We don't want to worry anyone, but those who are still thinking "I got vaccinated and have nothing to worry about": vaccine damage can occur immediately, after a few days or weeks, but also after several months or even years. In this respect it is like cancer: it can develop at lightning speed, but also very slowly.

Chapter 3: Unreported vaccine deaths?

*In just over a month, nearly 4,000 more deaths -
Spontaneous abortions after vaccinations in Great
Britain up 630% (relatively even up 3300%)*

The number of Covid-19 vaccine-induced deaths in the
EU had risen to 15,472 by June 19. Nearly 600,000
people suffered serious consequences, including
autoimmune diseases, disabilities (including deafness
and blindness), heart, kidney and liver problems, and
nervous system and muscle/bone disorders. Over one
and a half million people experienced milder, as yet not
permanent side effects. Vaccinations also have other
painful consequences: in Great Britain, the number of
spontaneous abortions after vaccination rose by 630%,
and relatively by as much as 3300%.

The official EMA figures have been showing all year that
the Covid-19 vaccinations have an extremely high
casualty rate everywhere, more than all other
vaccinations in the past 10 years combined. Despite
this, people are still eager to have this by far most
dangerous needle ever inserted into their arm. Why?
Because then they are rid of the "nagging" from their
employers or family and can be "free" again. At least,
that is the thought, because it is promoted so by the
media and politicians.

**In just over a month, almost 4,000 more deaths and
284,000 more serious cases**

Since our last book, published in June, the number of vaccine deaths has risen by 3953, and the number of people with serious (/ permanent) consequences by 284,187, almost doubling.

And this for supposedly fighting a virus that, even measured numerically over two seasons, is still comparable to a solid flu, and for 70-somethings even to a mild flu. (Average IFR from Covid is still only 0.15%, according to the world's top immunologist and WHO consultant Professor John Ioannidis. For 70-somethings, that's 0.05%, the HUGE of a normal flu).

The Moderna vaccine is the most dangerous with 8.41% deaths per report, followed by Johnson & Johnson (4.8%), Pfizer (3.11%) and AstraZeneca (1.15%). The Johnson vaccine produces the greatest number of adverse effects (3.0 per report), followed by AstraZeneca (2.7), Moderna (2.5) and Pfizer (2.3). Moderna's (55.91%) and AstraZeneca's (55.32%) vaccines produce the most severe symptoms. Pfizer follows with 41.96%, and Johnson with 33.77%.

Despite sectarian belief in 'science,' more and more meddling

Most reports come from the Netherlands (13.7%), followed by Italy (12%) and France (8.6%). However, it is quite conceivable that registration in the Netherlands is better and more accurate than in other countries, and many vaccine victims there do not end up in the statistics. Nevertheless, we know from direct sources that even in the Netherlands there are doctors who, even without having done any research, are able to immediately tell people who report side effects by phone that it 'cannot possibly be due to your vaccination'.

Talk about a blind and sectarian belief in 'science' - or what should pass for science these days! However, it is also possible that these doctors are simply too afraid of the consequences for their position and career if they report or register (serious) consequences of vaccinations as such, and therefore choose to 'put their money where their mouth is'.

Only 1% to 13% end up in statistics

The U.S. authorities admitted as recently as 2011 that only 1% to 13% of the number of vaccine victims are reported to the FDA. If we apply these figures to Europe, then in reality between 10 and 100 times more civilians would be affected than stated in these statistics, or between 6 and 60 million, not including 15,000+ deaths, but at least 150,000. (1)

Moreover, these are only the people for whom a direct link can be demonstrated, while it is scientifically known that many people only experience adverse health effects after several months, or even years. A causal link can then no longer be demonstrated directly.

Spontaneous abortions Great Britain increased by 630%

Vaccinations also have other painful consequences: in Great Britain the number of spontaneous abortions after vaccination has risen by 630%, and relatively speaking by as much as 3300%. Already 200 pregnant women lost their unborn child shortly after their Covid gene manipulation injection; 3 women did not survive it themselves.

Women who lose their unborn child after vaccination can hold their health care providers directly responsible, as the package insert and care instructions of, for example, the Pfizer 'vaccine' explicitly state that the injection should not be given to pregnant women, and women who want to become pregnant should wait at least 2 months after their vaccination to do so.

As in India, Chile, Taiwan and the Seychelles, the number of deaths has also exploded in the US and Great Britain after the start of the mass vaccination campaign against Covid-19. In less than 5 months, there have been more official vaccine deaths in the US than in the past 10 years (!). According to the VAERS registration system - which historically records only 1% to a maximum of 10% of the actual number of cases - over 1750 people died from vaccines in the first 3 months. That number currently stands at 5997. In the past week alone, 700 people died after being vaccinated against Covid-19.

Already 19,597 people were hospitalized after being vaccinated. 15,052 people had a severe allergic reaction. Another 43,891 people needed emergency medical attention. 2190 people had a heart attack, 1564 had thrombosis / blood clots / too low a level of platelets, 652 women had a miscarriage, and 4583 people were disabled.

More than 2 times as many deaths among vaccinated people

A 'vax horror massacre' is also taking place in Great Britain. The figures (Public Health England / UK National Health Service) are staggering: the number of deaths among vaccinated people is twice as high in percentage terms as among unvaccinated people.

Of the 19,573 unvaccinated who would have received the "delta" variant - which the mainstream media is of course again exploiting for yet another fear terror campaign - 23 people died (= mortality rate 0.00117%), including the "unlinked" category (4289 cases, bringing mortality rate to 0.00096%).

Of the 9344 vaccinated who received the delta mutation, 19 died (= mortality rate 0.00246%), more than twice as high as the unvaccinated, and more than 2.5 times as high if the 'unlinked' cases are also

19

included. 7 of the 19 deceased vaccinees died after 21 days or more after their first injection, and 12 of them died 14 days or more after their second shot, directly implicating the vaccine as a direct cause.

Warnings experts were ignored

The trend confirms the warnings of numerous scientists and experts such as the professor Pierre Capel, who has been warning since the autumn of 2020 that exactly this was about to happen what is now visible in more and more countries: vaccinated people who are subsequently infected with the virus or a mutation are much more likely than unvaccinated people to get ADE (Antibody Dependent Enhancement), a consequent serious illness or even death.

Celebrated scientists such as HIV-discoverer and Nobel laureate Luc Montagnier, and in Europe, Professor Schetters, have hammered away in vain at the fact that until 2020 it was an undisputed scientific fact that vaccinating during a pandemic is the most stupid thing you can ever do, because you create potentially dangerous mutations, which in turn increases the number of sick and dead.

However, politics never seemed to be about health or safety, but about injecting everyone as enforced as possible with experimental genetically modified organisms / gene therapy, as part of the technocratic transhuman totalitarian control agenda now being imposed on the world's population under various names (Great Reset, Agenda-2030, Build Back Better, Green New Deal).

'American companies count on losing MANY of their vaccinated employees'

American radio host Hal Turner has posted a video for subscribers that purports to show that American companies are counting on losing HALF of their vaccinated employees to a Covid-19 vaccine (dead or disabled). This information cannot be verified at this time.

Chapter 4: Proof of planning?

The possible reaction of the parties involved is entirely predictable: 'Coincidence'

A Confidential Agreement between the U.S. National Institutes of Allergies and Infectious Diseases (NIAID) and vaccine manufacturer Moderna would show that as early as December 12, 2019, it was agreed to transfer "potential coronavirus vaccine candidates" to the University of North Carolina. That was 19 days BEFORE the first report of a new virus in Wuhan, China. If this document is authentic, it is another strong indication that we are indeed dealing with a planned pandemic, or plandemic. The next question then arises: are these parties then also the causal agents of the coronavirus "outbreak"?

The document was signed by Ralph Baric (PhD) of the University of North Carolina (Chapel Hill) on December 12, 2019. Baric later surfaced in some media as the "UNC coronavirus expert.

The other signatory is Jacqueline Quay, Director of Licensing and Innovation Support at the same university. Her signature is dated December 16, 2019. Until 2009, Quay was director of Intellectual Property at the Duke Human Vaccine Institute and the Center for HIV-AIDS Vaccine Immunology (CHAVI) located there.

On behalf of the supplier of the mRNA coronavirus vaccine candidates, Barney Graham MD (PhD) also signed the document. Graham is an "investigator" at NIAID. An electronic signature, dated December 12, is from Amy F. Petrik, Technology Transfer Specialist. Finally, there is the scrawl of Moderna researcher Sunny Himansu (PhD). The whole thing was approved by attorney Shaun Ryan, Moderna's Deputy General Counsel.

How did the US and Moderna know about the coronavirus almost 3 weeks in advance?

So all these people were aware well before there was an outbreak in China that an mRNA coronavirus vaccine would be needed, and that the best candidate had to be chosen. How could both the U.S. medical authorities and Moderna have known this? It was not until December 31 that there was the first small report of a new virus in Wuhan. The WHO timeline clearly states that it was only on that date that "a new viral pneumonia" had emerged in Wuhan.

Turner wonders aloud whether it is not time for a thorough investigation into the real causative agents of the corona p(l)andemic. But what do you do when the (co-)culprits (U.S. government) themselves start conducting that investigation? The NIAID director is a Dr. Anthony Fauci, who appears to have told nothing but lies in the past year, and whose direct link to the 'gain of function' coronavirus research in Wuhan has been proven (1). Can any official research be trusted at all in the year 2021?

Event 201 planned 65 million deaths

This foreknowledge of the coronavirus is, of course, easy to explain in light of the now infamous Event 201 in October 2019, when extensive rehearsals were held with various agencies and governments for a 'possible' global outbreak with a coronavirus, which is 'planned' to kill 65 million people. During Event 201, the scenario was described as being followed exactly since 2020. We are now in the 'intermediate' phase, where it seems that the virus is disappearing. However, this will be followed by a double whammy of return (presumably in the fall/winter), from which, according to the scenario, tens of millions 'must' die.

The eventual reaction of the parties involved and the media to this paper is entirely predictable:

'Yes, we had been working on a coronavirus vaccine for years. It is pure coincidence that this document was signed so shortly before the outbreak.'

I don't really have hope anymore that people will finally wake up to what is really going on. The attitude of most people is now so docile and naive that if the government and the media tell them that the sky is not blue but pink, they will take this at face value. The price that will have to be paid in the coming years for this uninterested, indifferent and insignificant attitude could, however, be sky-high.

Chapter 5: Mass murder?

'Everything the government and their scientists have told us over the past year and a half, whether it's about lockdowns, infections, face masks, deaths or mutations, are outright lies' - 'The chances of vaccinated people coming away from this unscathed? ZERO' - If you want to kill billions of people over the course of months or years and have 'plausible deniability', this is THE way'

Dr. Mike Yeadon, ex-vice president and CSO Allergy and Respiratory Research at Pfizer, as a top immunologist, has been one of the most outspoken opponents of mass corona vaccinations over the past year. He says people "don't have to be afraid of this virus, but they do have to be terrified of their own government. Because everything you've been told about lockdowns, infections, face masks or mutations have been outright lies.' He warned earlier that mRNA vaccines are potential bioweapons. 'If you wanted to wipe out the world's population (without being able to be directly blamed), this is the way.' He doesn't take back a word of that.

In an interview with The Highwire, Yeadon says he found it very suspicious when a lockdown was declared in March 2020, and he was downright shocked when the government decided to extend that lockdown, despite the fact that the morbidity and mortality figures did not justify it at all. 'That's when I knew there was absolutely something incredibly wrong. People should not be afraid of this virus. Everything that the government and their scientists have been telling us for the past year and a half are lies. That is not just an opinion, but a fact. They are deliberately telling untruths, and we call those lies.'

'Purpose: to make us ripe for vaccines, which is a very serious crime'

'The goal was to make us ripe for the vaccines... I think a very serious crime is being committed.' Yeadon points to WHO advisor and the world's top immunologist John Ioannidis, who confirmed last year that 'this corona pandemic is comparable in every way to a solid seasonal flu, and no worse. So the best epidemiologist in the world judges that it is only a little bit worse than a typical flu.'

'But the government and all the policy makers are giving the impression that this virus is unprecedented (dangerous), which is simply not true. What makes me especially angry is that good medicines (HCQ, Ivermectin, etc.) are being denied to people. They said there are no treatments, and that is definitely not true.' Numerous medics and scientists worldwide have proven that these drugs are actually excellent against Covid-19 (in various stages). 'If these drugs had been made available, we would have been rid of it in a few months.'

Falsely used PCR test totally unreliable for this purpose

Yeadon also points again to the PCR test, which has long been known to be totally unsuitable for demonstrating virus infection, as the inventor (and Nobel laureate) said back in 2019, and which was even acknowledged by Marion Koopmans late last year. Moreover, this PCR test is also not used according to the scientific standard. So many cycles are used (40-45, while 20-25 times is the absolute maximum), that the test results are completely unreliable (95% false positives), and every residue of whatever virus - including a common cold - gives a 'positive' result.

According to the ex-Pfizer VP, this was done intentionally to be able to 'demonstrate' the highest possible number of (fake) infections, in order to justify the lockdown measures. Moreover, the PCR test never shows whether someone is sick or infectious (contagious to others) anyway. (The infection rates on the various corona dashboards were and are therefore utterly bogus).

'People without symptoms are NEVER contagious'

This was followed by yet another glass-hard lie, namely that people without symptoms could be contagious. 'I knew this wasn't true. This is my expertise! This has been my job for 40 years. They know I'm right. Only people with lots of virus particles in their airways are contagious. However, those will always have symptoms. There is no debate about that. People without symptoms therefore have few virus particles, and therefore cannot infect others. There is a lot of literature on that.' Even Anthony 'lying' Fauci literally admitted as much in February 2020.

'I accuse the advisers and the ministers of mass murder'

'Over the course of the year I came to the conclusion - and this is a hard assertion - that literally everything the government and their experts tell you is all lies. Yes, people died, presumably tens of thousands. But they probably could have been saved. So I accuse the government's scientific advisors and ministers of mass murder. I want to see them in the dock.'

'For those who believe that the government has told you the truth, this is a big turning point. I realize this is a big shock.'

Media are 'horrible liars,' because risk of contagion is zero

He points to a scientific study that showed that people with a positive PCR test but no symptoms only have a maximum 0.7% chance of infecting someone in their own household. So the risk of infection was and still is zero.

'I also blame the media, what horrible liars they are! They are damaging their own society and lives, including those of their children. For months they have lied to us that you can pass this virus on to others without noticing. That is an outright lie, and simply impossible.'

Another huge lie: the face masks, which everyone has to wear. If you have no symptoms, a mouth mask is nonsense anyway, 'but absolutely harmful' to your health. So what do face masks do? Keep the deliberately sown fear among people alive and fueling it. That is the main reason: to scare people to death. That fits in with the other lies they tell you.'

Lockdowns have made no difference, infections take place in institutions

Lockdowns, which restricted all human contact, never work and are useless. In a respiratory virus epidemic, it's only about the number of infectious contacts, i.e., people with symptoms of illness who can infect others. But we have known how to deal with that since time immemorial: stay at home! And you limit the number of contacts automatically, because you are sick and/or have a fever. The few people who get really, really sick end up in hospital.

And that's why closing down companies and the like hasn't made any difference. That's not where the infections took place. Where did they occur? In the places where there are many people with symptoms, and at the same time many people who are susceptible: hospitals! And what do you think? A lot of infections did occur there, just like in nursing homes. In families much less, because there was already much existing immunity, and children cannot spread the virus.'

'I believe 90% of all infections occurred in those institutions. The same thing happened with SARS-1 in 2003, and MERS in 2012. Also, SARS-CoV-2 is primarily a disease that occurs in institutions. So your government lied to you. Lockdowns could never have worked, because the infections occurred in institutions, not in society.'

Variants and mutations differ by at most 0.3%, all humans are immune to it

'So that's a whole list of lies we've been told, from the exaggeration of mortality rates to the claims that there are no treatments. Oh yes, and another one: that this is a 'novel' (new) virus, and so no one has immunity. The whole world became terrified. I then did research and saw that this virus is 80% similar to SARS-1 (2003), and about 60% similar to a common coronavirus cold. So I thought: nice, nothing to worry about. Immunology is my strong suit, and so I WISHED that a lot of people already had very strong immunity (T-cells and antibodies).'

The scientific advisors to our governments know this too. One of the official British advisors, Sr. Patrick Vallance (the British Jaap van Dissel), is even a former colleague of Yeadon. We had the same textbooks and the same training. I'm sure he knows what I know, and that when this is over, he will confirm all my points, because they are scientifically so clear. Unfortunately, he and other advisors have repeatedly lied outright, and that is to scare people.'

'Now the next lie, the one in 2021: variants (mutations).' People get terms like the 'Brazilian' or 'Indian' or 'Delta' variant that 'these are really very different, otherwise government and media wouldn't say anything about that, would they? But I looked at it carefully. The variant that differs the most from the one from Wuhan differs only by 0.3%. In other words, it is 99.7% the same, or more. So it is impossible that these variants could evade human immunity. Impossible. What they tell you about this are lies.'

'I am ashamed of the scientists who support these lies'

Yeadon says he is ashamed of that part of the scientists who continue to sell and support all these lies with manipulated studies and reports. 'There is no doubt that a variant that differs by only 0.3% does not cause disease symptoms in anyone (with immunity). Impossible! As a scientist, it is very frustrating to hear how ministers and advisors talk to the media about variants. They are lying their asses off! Because I understand how this works. Both theoretically and empirically, this is not possible. They are not different enough to worry about.'

He points to a scientific study (published on bioRXiv, from Cold Spring Harbor Laboratory) that found that human T cells respond to ALL variants. The scientists who dared to publish this 'are national heroes. Their research told me what I needed to know to say this to you now.'

'Absurd that the media won't allow a critical voice'

Interviewer Del Bigtree asks him why none of the policymakers will listen to him. Yeadon replies that he is definitely not the only one, that he and other scientists, doctors and experts started writing articles and doing research, and trying to get on TV with their visions and conclusions to reflect a different point of view. But not one broadcaster wants critical scientists like him to speak. 'Really absurd.

'How can scientists involved in this still sleep?'

I don't understand how the scientists involved can still sleep at night... When I look at these gene-based 'vaccines' as a toxicologist, they all contain a genetic code for the spike protein of the virus. It took me 5 minutes to find 3 studies. One study says that the spike protein causes blood clots; another that it can cause a cytokine storm.'

'I remember being filled with horror when I read that. 'So you put something in these vaccines that makes people's bodies make (countless) copies of this spike

33

protein? That couldn't exist, could it? Because this causes toxins (toxins) to be produced in your own body! For a few days I thought maybe they had changed the spike protein so it wouldn't be harmful anymore, but then I realized they hadn't.'

'As a toxicologist, I knew people were going to die'

The former Pfizer top executive then quotes Dr Sucharit Bhakdi, a highly regarded award-winning researcher with more than 300 publications in immunology and virology to his name. 'In November I had a long telephone conversation with him. We both unfortunately came to the same conclusion: ALL these vaccines cause the body to produce this spike protein, and it is impossible for these substances to remain only at the injection site (which has been claimed for months by government, manufacturers and media, but which has proven to be a demonstrable lie).'

'So we were sure that some people would get blood clots.' Together with Bhakdi, among others, and another renowned critical expert, Dr. Wolfgang Wodarg, as 'Doctors for Covid Ethics' they unsuccessfully submitted a number of open letters and petitions to the EMA in Amsterdam to stop these vaccines. 'As a toxicologist, I knew that people were going to die because of this, which I was very upset about.'

'There has been NO research into what this non-natural chemical is doing in your body'

All the scientific publications of the last 10 years show
that mRNA was far from being ready to be used en
masse in (gene therapy) vaccines for humans.
Numerous problems were and ARE still not solved.

'What I'm about to tell you a lot of people don't know
yet. When these gene-based 'vaccines' are given to you,
you are getting a foreign, modified and non-natural
chemical agent into your body. They should have done
toxicological studies on that, but nobody did! So I
couldn't believe that the agencies still gave their
approval for testing on tens of thousands of people.
They didn't even have the basics in place yet! Then how
could they know that these chemicals would not be
toxic?'

'As a pharmacologist, I want to know what a drug does
in the body of a human or animal, where it goes in the
body, and how long it remains active. Vaccine
manufacturers are NOT required to do this research. So
they have NOT studied where the vaccine/spike protein
goes in your body once it is injected, how much of it
gets into your body, and how long it stays there. I was
almost in tears when I read that file, because they have
NO idea what will happen.'

'The chances of vaccinated people getting out of this
unscathed are zero'

'But I can tell you this: mother nature is never so kind when you introduce something new, when you inject a brand new chemical into a human being, and you haven't researched where it's going to go and what it's going to do. The chances of you getting away with this unscathed? ZERO. Just not going to happen.' In other words: ANY vaccinated person is going to experience health damage from this sooner or later.

'These are the most dangerous vaccines ever. Remember that I am normally very positive about new vaccine developments, I have spent my life working on them. But I am also very much in favor of safety.' The (supposed) operation of these new mRNA vaccines contains no less than 5 steps. During each step, something can and WILL go wrong. Some people will experience only mild damage, others very severe.

During his own time at Pfizer, mRNA already proved very difficult to work with. 'The idea that in just 10 years this will suddenly be safe enough to be used in humans is impossible. It just doesn't work that way.' (As recently as 2019, scientists from America's top universities collectively concluded that it would be many years before it could possibly be established that mRNA (vaccines/therapy) is safe enough to inject into people.)

Then follows a discussion of a recent study by systems scientists that attempted to prove that vaccines pose no danger to pregnant women. Yeadon explains, using statistics from that study, that the conclusions are wrong, and that there is a danger - admittedly not much, but certainly not zero, according to him. He calls what is being done now - only investigating the possible consequences AFTER people have already been vaccinated - 'reckless'.

'ADEs can lead to huge numbers of deaths'

The same goes for Covid vaccinations in general. 'We have injected healthy people with something that can harm them (such as creating blood clots).' Many people have also been found to be allergic to the adjuvant PEC in the vaccines. 'And guess what? On the very first day of vaccination in my country (Great Britain), two care workers went into anaphylactic shock. According to your VAERS system, thousands and thousands of people have already had such an anaphylactic reaction. And it's still going on.'

'So far, the liars have been wrong every time. But I'm afraid the end is not yet in sight. You already mentioned ADE (Antibody Dependent Enchancement). If that occurs, it could be catastrophic, and literally lead to huge numbers of deaths. Some doctors are already predicting this, and I am as concerned as they are. I just can't assess how likely this is.'

'All these lies are, at the very least, hard evidence of international cooperation'

75% - 80% of the population gets vaccinated, 'but nothing at all is known about long-term safety. So what happens when things go wrong? You start to wonder if someone is indeed trying to kill large numbers of people. All the lies that are being told do seem to indicate this.'

'In 2018 or 2015 we would never have done all these things. Everything was conceived all at once and spread around the world in 2020. ALL governments started spreading the same lies at the same time. If anyone can explain to me even then that this is all a coincidence? Come on! At the very least, this is hard evidence of international cooperation, at the supranational level. So in February (2020) there was already a plan to deceive you.'

'If your government does something stupid and illegal, you have two choices'

'I tell people: if your government does something that is a) stupid, and b) illegal, you have two choices. One: you go along with it, or two: you stand up and fight it. And it is so stupid! Suppose I was vaccinated, then I don't need to know if you or someone else is vaccinated too, do I? I'm protected, aren't I? If I were to get the virus, it would be destroyed, right?

'Then why do you have to show a vaccine passport? Who want that? The people who want you to take that vaccine are people like (Tony) Blair, Bill Gates and others. Blair resigned with a scandal, is a war criminal, and I think has remained so. He is a politician, I am a scientist. I'm absolutely convinced that no one will benefit from these vaccine passports... It's mind-boggling that the media doesn't even wonder about this, because if they did, they would realize that it doesn't work, that it's a stupid idea.'

But what is happening in the meantime? People everywhere are being put under great pressure, indirectly forced, to get vaccinated - including in the Netherlands. That is coercion, and it is not permitted to force people to undergo a medical procedure, and certainly not an experimental one. That is explicitly forbidden in the Nuremberg Code and international law, which has been signed by all countries. But still they do it.'

'Digital vaccine passports give government total control over you'

'So what I'm saying is: don't take Covid-19 vaccines! And as for vaccine passports, I can't think of anything in my 61 years of age that is more important than preventing this system from coming into being. Because if we let ourselves be fooled into thinking we have to have one of those apps on our phone to prove you've been vaccinated, then you'll get the first global general digital ID, there will be no more borders, and they can stop you for doing anything (or getting anywhere).'

'If this system comes in, anyone who owns this database will have complete control over you. Then they can ban you from getting on airplanes, stores or gas stations. They will have total control over you, and if they think you should not do something, they will stop you, and there is nothing you can do about it. Because everyone around you is participating, and you have no choice.'

'The whole purpose of this pandemic, the lies and the vaccines is to get you on this digital ID. Once this system is up and running, they will force you on 'booster shots' (new vaccinations) with lies about mutations. You do NOT need these; I am terrified of these 'booster shots'. These are not vaccines. Billions of doses of them are already being made.'

'What will happen then? Then you'll get a message on your smartphone telling you to go get this or that vaccine within 2 weeks. You don't? Then your vaccination passport will expire, and with it, your payment card to get into a store or gas station. I'm not saying this will happen, but it could. There is enough evidence that some very evil players are involved.'

'And what now if the next vaccines contain something to kill you?'

'And now what if in the third, fourth or fifth vaccine there is something designed to kill you? I don't know, but if I wanted to set up a system with total control and plausible deniability, and inject into billions of people something that kills them over the course of months or years, I can't think of a better plan than this.'

'If you think: you have gone mad - show me wherein I am not logical. Because otherwise you are relying on people who are actually that bad. And I'm afraid those people exist. There have always been those, look at Pol Pot, the Nazis, Stalin, Argentina in the 1970s. Over time, there have been people everywhere who are willing to kill other people to get their way. All I'm suggesting now is that this is happening now too. The only difference is that this time it's happening with technology instead of weapons, and because of the Internet just about everyone on this planet is involved.'

'But apart from that, it's the same corrupt, repugnant people with criminal minds. I think they have now come up with this system that allows this to happen. And even if you believe the government: please never agree to digital vaccine passports so they can have total control over you and later force you to get injected. Immunologists say these can't be vaccines - so what are they?'

These are mass murderers who don't care about a zero.

I am not a religious person, but I have come to the conclusion that I am now looking at the faces of Evil. People can steal, cheat, break in, people can do evil things. But THIS plan was not devised in 5 minutes... If someone is willing to sign (or execute) an order (/ law) that they know will cost, say, 20,000 people their lives, then you have already decided that you are a mass murderer, and it doesn't matter anymore if a few more zeros are added to that and it becomes NINE zeros (a billion).'

'Those who are hearing this for the first time will think I'm going crazy, but I'm as calm as I can be. We were lied to about the severity of the virus, which is not that dangerous at all. Effective medications were denied us. Measures such as lockdowns and facemasks are patently ineffective. Also, the narrative about variants (/ mutations) is not true. So even if the vaccine did turn out to be safe, you are still being misled with this narrative to what I believe are the gates of hell.'

'If anyone doesn't want to believe this: I have yet to come across anyone who has a benign explanation for what is being done now. My conclusions as to where this is leading may be wrong, but not my conclusions that this is being done misleadingly and deliberately, and that it is hurting people.'

'Be terrified of your government, and take back your freedom'

'As far as the virus is concerned, there is little you need to be afraid of. It has all but disappeared in the world. What you do have to be afraid of is your government...

People who don't read alternative news sources think
that what the government tells them is the truth. Be
terrified of your government; you MUST take back your
freedoms peacefully. They have to give it back to you,
because they did not take it from you in a lawful way...
and are now exposing you to very dangerous vaccines.'

*'So peacefully take back your freedom. If you don't, I
don't know where this is going to end, but it won't be
good.'*

Chapter 6: Heart inflammation?

*'Congratulations, you are destroying for a generation
ALL trust in ALL vaccines' - 'Number of cases of
myocarditis and pericarditis 40 times higher than
normal'*

The U.S. CDC is holding an 'emergency' meeting about
the 'unexpectedly' very high numbers of children and
adolescents who have developed heart inflammation
after being injected with a Covid-19 'vaccine' from Pfizer
or Moderna. 'Urgency' in quotes, because the meeting
is not for another 7 days. In the meantime, parents are
still urged to simply take their children (ages 12 and up)
to an injection site. Yale economist-historian and award
winning ex-New York Times journalist and author Alex
Berenson reacts furiously: "You stupid, stupid fools. This
was all so predictable.'

The myocarditis (heart muscle inflammation) and
pericarditis (pericardium inflammation) 'epidemic' is
occurring mostly among young men and teenage boys
(ages 16 - 24) who have been vaccinated for the second
time. Recently, the CDC asked health care providers to
ask patients with symptoms of heart inflammation if
they had recently been vaccinated against Covid-19.

**800 reported heart infections, but presumably many
more**

The VAERS database that tracks the 800 heart infections has been updated to May 31, so in the meantime the number of adolescents and children who have been affected by this thanks to their vaccination will only have grown.

Moreover, historically only 1% to a maximum of 10% of the actual number of vaccine victims are included in this database. This is partly because people who still become (deathly) ill or die some time later after their vaccination are no longer counted, and doctors and researchers (as in Europe and the rest of the world) are heavily discouraged from linking cases of illness to a vaccination, even if it has only just been administered.

People who get myocarditis usually have to be hospitalized. Of 285 registered patients, 270 are now said to have been sent home again. 15 of them are still in the hospital. Normally, only 2 to 19 children aged 16 and 17 'should' have contracted myocarditis, but the actual number (up to May 31) is 79. For the age group 18- 24, the 'accepted' number is 8 to 83, but in reality 196 people were affected.

The FDA recorded 42 cases of myocarditis/pericarditis in the 42 days after vaccination in 3.1 million people between 12 and 64 years old. Among those over 65, the number was 1260. Federal officials and concerned medics consider the numbers of adverse reactions, although many times higher than normal in all areas, still "acceptable," and so the general expectation is that vaccination will continue as usual. The only consideration is to give children up to 20 years of age only one shot, or to reduce the dose, or to lengthen the time between injections.

'Congratulations, you are destroying ALL confidence in ALL vaccines for a generation'

Berenson, author of "Tell Your Children: The Truth about Marijuana, Mental Illness and Violence," among other books, is appalled at the authorities: "Congratulations, you morons. You are about to destroy a generation's worth of ALL confidence in ALL vaccines and ALL public health measures.'

Well, that trust has long since disappeared in a growing number of people, Mr. Berenson, as evidenced by the fact that Americans have had to be persuaded lately with free lotto tickets, bonuses and all sorts of prize festivals to go get their 'shots.

Berens analyzed all the statistics, concluding that the incidence of heart disease among children and adolescents is as much as 40 times higher than normal. 'And consider that most side effects are not reported, even if they are serious.'

The author writes of being behind a lawsuit by a student who is suing his private school for demanding that all students be vaccinated against Covid-19. One reader has reportedly already offered $25,000 in support. Across the U.S., numerous schools and universities are already mandating vaccinations.

Israel: 275 cases

On the same day (June 1), the Israeli Ministry of Health reported 275 cases of heart infection (again, mostly young men aged 16 - 30) out of more than 5 million vaccinations. This may seem small, but the same misleading registration system is used here: only people who become ill shortly after their vaccination are counted, even though it has long been scientifically known that people can become ill as a result of vaccinations several months or even years later.

Chapter 7: Vaccine restrictions?

Air travel for ordinary people has been a thorn in the side of the globalist climate-vaccine cult for years. Now, it seems, steps are actually being taken to put an end to it once and for all under the guise of "health" and "safety. Vaccinated people have increased risk of brain hemorrhage or heart attack and European pilots are locked in hotel rooms despite vaccinations.

Airlines in Spain and Russia have begun to warn vaccinated people not to get on a plane. They may even be hit with a no-fly zone. The reason is that vaccinated people are at extra risk of blood clots (DVT: Deep Vein Thrombosis) in high-altitude pressurized cabins, and can therefore suffer a brain hemorrhage or heart attack more quickly.

The US CDC has a general warning on its website for people who travel longer than four hours by plane: "More than 300 million people travel annually on long-haul flights (usually more than four hours). Blood clots, also called DVT (deep vein thrombosis), can be a serious risk for some long-distance travelers... Anyone who travels for more than four hours, whether by plane, car, bus or train, may be at risk of blood clots.

The end for almost ALL travel?

That the car, bus and train have now been added to that list (in which there are no pressurized cabins) makes many people wonder whether the globalist climate-vaccine sect intends, under the guise of 'health' and 'the climate', to put an end to almost ALL travel (except for themselves, of course).

Initially, the plan was to allow only vaccinated people to have access to international flights again. Now that it turns out that they are actually at increased risk, the question arises whether it was indeed not the intention from the outset to put an end to at least 90% of air travel.

Pilots are locked up in hotel rooms despite vaccinations

Despite their vaccinations, pilots and other crew members in Europe are locked in hotel rooms immediately upon arrival at an airport. In most cases, they are not allowed to leave the airport. In March, the European Aviation Safety Agency (EASA) recommended that vaccinated pilots also be quarantined for at least two days before boarding.

Since vaccinated pilots spend much longer "in the air" and they are therefore at even greater risk, this raises the question of whether air travel has not become permanently more unsafe.

Australian airlines deny there is greater risk

American economist Martin Armstrong writes of having a friend who was vaccinated against Covid, and then suffered a blood clot that he had to have surgically removed.

According to the UK Evening Standard, the risk is the same for vaccinated and unvaccinated people. Australian airlines claim it's not true at all, and you can just fly if you're vaccinated. 'Of course they are not interested in people's safety,' Armstrong responds. 'They just want to stay afloat. There have been recorded deaths from blood clots after people were vaccinated, without flying. Others have found that Covid deaths often had blood clots.'

'Politicians will never admit their mistakes; there is no one left whom we can trust'

'As with everything around Covid, there is no real hard information. We probably won't get any either, because the government is pushing the vaccine through. Politicians will NEVER admit their mistakes, no matter how many people die. They can't be prosecuted, because they control the whole (judicial) process, and the media doesn't help either.'

Armstrong writes that he would rather remain normal. *'If I never have to leave my house again - fine. I've had enough of this deranged world anyway. I will patiently wait for the mushroom cloud that removes the threat to humanity and signals that it is all over. There is simply no one left in the authorities whom we can trust.'*

Chapter 8: The US and China working together?

Why did China NOT use the challenged mRNA/DNA technology in its own vaccines? - NIH director: 'SARS-1 and MERS also come from there'

And yet another 'conspiracy theory' that turns out to be a hard fact, thereby exposing yet another lie perpetuated for months by the mainstream media and politicians. Dr. Francis Collins, the current director of the American National Institutes of Health (NIH), has frankly admitted in an interview that the Americans and the Chinese collaborated to make the coronavirus more contagious to humans ('gain of function') in the biohazard-4 lab in Wuhan. Dr. Anthony Fauci, who is in ever greater trouble because of his many lies that have now been proven, denied to the Senate in March that he and his colleague Collins had funded the "gain of function" research in the Wuhan lab. Now he appears to have committed perjury about that.

'SARS and MERS come from there'

Collins' statements are also highly incriminating for Dr. Peter Daszak, who through his Ecohealth Alliance received substantial grants from the NIH to fund the 'gain of function' research in Wuhan. Collins explained in detail how the NIH and the Wuhan Institute of Virology work together. He insisted that there is 'good reason' for this, as both SARS-1 and MERS 'originated there'.

Mike 'Natural News' Adams hears in this that both SARS and MERS come from the Wuhan laboratory, but in my opinion by 'there' Collins meant China in general. Indeed, SARS-1 first surfaced in China in 2003. Its spread was subsequently limited to four other countries.

However, MERS was first detected in Saudi Arabia in 2012 (see also our article yesterday: Medical journals announce potential new pandemic: MERS-CoV). Adams is therefore right to wonder, after all, if "Collins has more information that these relatively new and deadly coronaviruses (SARS, MERS) both came from the Wuhan lab?

Conspiracy theory turns out to be hard fact

Dr. Collins, Daszak and Fauci worked directly with the infamous 'bat lady' Dr. Shi Zhengli, who is funded and rewarded by the Chinese Communist Party (CCP), according to press reports from the Wuhan lab. The Wuhan Institute of Virology is also the center of a 'United Front Group' established to neutralize all potential opposition and criticism of the CCP. When the lab was identified as a possible source of the coronavirus last year, China blocked a WHO investigation into it. Then, for months, Dr. Fauci proclaimed the now-proven crystal-clear lies, and even committed perjury about it.

53

The same applies to Dr. Daszak, regularly quoted in Western media, who kept insisting that an artificial origin of the virus, i.e. a "lab leak" - intentional or otherwise - was a "conspiracy theory". Scientists who pointed out the many inconsistencies and factual evidence that the bat soup or seafood market theory, also accepted as 'true' in Europe, is pure nonsense, were virulently attacked and blackened. This even happened to HIV-discoverer and Nobel Prize winner Luc Montagnier.

Walking 'COVID factories'

Fauci, Daszak and other system scientists have also gone all out to inject the entire world population with experimental genetic manipulation "vaccines," which have now been shown to turn people into walking "spike factories" that are also "shed" (exhaled) into the environment. In previous articles we pointed out the growing number of scientific studies and reports that those exhaled 'spikes' can also cause damage to the health of unvaccinated people.

If that is placed in the light of the leaked 'Fauci Files', from which it emerged that the coronavirus was already referred to internally as a deliberately created 'bioweapon' on March 11, 2020, then a terrifying picture emerges that is probably too much for most people to take in all at once.

Chinese vaccines contain no mRNA - why not there, and here?

Consider the following: soon after the outbreak of the corona pandemic, China shared all the information about the (supposed) SARS-CoV-2 virus with the world, including the complete genetic construction plan. Based on this, new vaccines based on mRNA and DNA technology, never used or tested on humans, were developed in America, Europe, Russia and India, with which the largest medical experiment in history is now being conducted by injecting as many people and even children as possible with it.

However, the Chinese vaccines do not contain this mRNA/DNA technology. There, the society and economy have been running normally for quite some time. What could be the reason that the Chinese did not want to inject mRNA instructions into their population? Were they perhaps fully aware of the gigantic risks that would entail?

An even more important question: why was and is it done here?

Chapter 9: No escape?

Member of Canadian government unveiled global roadmap to totalitarian communism in October 2020 in which no one owns anything and everyone must be compulsorily vaccinated!

Yet another country confirming a particularly worrying trend: after the start of the Covid-19 vaccination campaign, the number of sick and dead explodes in Taiwan. The same thing happened before in India, Chile and Seychelles, among others, where more (AstraZeneca) shots were handed out than people live, after which there were 146 times more deaths in 4 months than from corona last year. And as we have been predicting for so long, the authorities refuse to point to the vaccines as the cause, no matter how obvious the statistical link. But the "vaccines" - excuse: experimental genetic gene therapy/manipulation - are now declared untouchable and sacrosanct, and so it is indeed claimed that it is due to a mutation.

Taiwan was rid of corona early this year. Hardly anyone died from Covid-19 anymore, there were hardly any sick people, and life returned to normal - except for the wretched mouth masks, which still had to be worn in public places. The reason for this can only be guessed at, as there was no medical one.

Despite the fact that the umpteenth respiratory virus was under control, the government still began a massive vaccination campaign. This got off to a very slow start in mid-March, but starting in May, the number of people getting injected with experimental mRNA/DNA manipulation suddenly skyrocketed.

EXACTLY at that moment the number of 'cases' and deaths also skyrocketed.

Member of Canadian government revealed road map to totalitarian communism in October

American radio host Hal Turner cites an October 2020 open letter from a member of the Canadian government, which we also published at the time. Here again the most important parts from it:

'I want to give you very important information. I am a committee member of the Liberal Party of Canada. I sit on various committee groups, but the information I give comes from the Strategic Plan Committee (which is controlled by the PMO).' That is the office of left-liberal Prime Minister Justin Trudeau, whose parliament has now given itself unlimited power and an unlimited term without an election as long as there is still a 'pandemic'. Trudeau has thus become Canada's de facto first dictator.

'They have made it very clear that nothing can stop their planned outcome. The roadmap and objectives were drawn up by the prime minister, and go as follows:' (planned time period: late 2020 - late 2021)

* 'Introduce second lockdown restrictions gradually.
Start with major urban areas first, and then expand;

* Obtain or build isolation facilities in each province at a
rapid pace;

* Rapidly increase the number of new 'Covid cases' and
'Covid deaths' so that there is no longer sufficient
testing capacity;

* Complete and total second lockdown in 2021, which is
much more severe than the first in spring 2020;

* Present the PLANNED Covid-19 mutation or
'reinfection' with a second virus (possibly called Covid-
21 (or perhaps SARS-3 or MERS-CoV)), leading to a
THIRD wave with a much higher mortality rate and even
higher infection rate;

* The health care system is flooded with Covid-19 /
Covid-21 patients;

* THIRD lockdown with even stricter measures, such as
a complete stop on ALL travel (second/third quarter
2021);

* Implement universal basic income (for the tens of
millions of new unemployed who will lose their jobs
permanently as a result of this policy. This UBI will be

completely digital, only allowing you to stay alive and watch TV);

* Supply lines collapse, major shortages (stores, supermarkets, online, etc.), major economic instability, followed by chaos, panic, and total dislocation;

* Deploy the military, and establish checkpoints on all major roads. Travel permanently extremely restricted (only by pass / permission). (Third / fourth quarter 2021).'

Depending on the geopolitical situation, the timeline could still change (e.g., 2021 could also be 2022 or 2023), but 'we have been told that in order to initiate this actual economic collapse on an international scale, the federal government is going to offer Canadians a total debt cancellation.' But that comes at a very high price: anyone who claims it gives up forever all rights to all forms of property, and commits to taking all vaccinations offered.

Refusers will initially have to live under very strict lockdown restrictions indefinitely, and thus stay home permanently. But that will only last for a short period, because once the majority of citizens have made the "transition" (to permanent slavery under a global totalitarian communist and transhumanist control system), "the refusers will be characterized as a threat to public safety, and moved to isolation facilities.
Or, in other words, to concentration camps.

There they will be given one last chance to still 'participate' in the program and have all vaccinations injected into them. If not, they will remain locked up permanently and lose all their possessions and rights. 'In the end, the Prime Minister implied that this whole agenda will be pushed through, regardless of whether we agree with it or not. And this is not just happening in Canada. All countries will have similar roadmaps and agendas. They want to take advantage of the situation to make large-scale changes' (a financial reset with IMF world currency, the 'Great Reset', 'Build Back Better', UN Agenda 2030, the 'Green New Deal').

After the purposefully initiated economic collapse, many of the tens of millions of unemployed system followers will be eager for a BOA-Sturmabteilung brown shirt job in the government, after which they will impose the above scenario on unwilling fellow citizens with ruthless cruelty. Friends, neighbors, colleagues, family and relatives, students and schoolchildren will betray each other "for the greater good," and will be happy that the "threats to their health" will be cleared away for good. (See also: This is how Reichsmarschall Göring got the people to say, "Scare them and tell them that refusers are a danger") and Corona policy tears families and friends apart, exactly as was done in GDR).

Precisely because most people still refuse to believe that this can and will never happen again, that we are more civilized nowadays and will never again commit such atrocities, it threatens to happen again. The only thing that can stop this whole process, this preconceived perfidious plan, is a massive awareness, followed by a massive (but we repeat: definitely non-violent!) NO.

Chapter 10: The next pandemic?

MERS-CoV had a 40% mortality rate in 2012 - African variant made contagious to humans through genetic engineering - Repeat of 2020, supplemented by mandatory testing and mandatory vaccinations for all? - Predictable: politics and media will blame unvaccinated people

Exactly according to the scenario we have described many times since last year, medical journals are announcing the next pandemic now that Covid-19 seems to be on its way out: MERS-CoV. We can therefore expect a repeat of everything from last year's deliberate scare-mongering to the disinformation propaganda in the mainstream media and a rush to the health care system, after which 'natural' measures will be taken such as new strict lockdowns, supplemented by mandatory testing and mandatory vaccinations for everyone. Because again, the main intention of this pandemic seems to be to inject everyone with yet another series of new experimental vaccines.

'Make no mistake, this will not be the last time the world faces the threat of a pandemic,' Tedros told the UN General Assembly of the health ministers of the 194 member states earlier this year. 'It is an evolutionary certainty that there will be another virus with the potential to be even more infectious and deadly than this one.'

Indeed, that other virus could already be coming. An international team of researchers has discovered that Middle East Respiratory Syndrome (MERS) is just a few mutations away from becoming a serious pandemic. In their paper, published in Proceedings of the National Academy of Sciences, they describe their research on several MERS variants.

MERS-CoV first surfaced in Saudi Arabia in 2012, and is said to be particularly deadly. About 40% of the first patients died from their infections, which were allegedly caused mainly by infected dromedaries. And coincidence or not, evidence was also found that bats had infected the camels. According to researchers, 80% of all dromedaries tested (70% live in Africa) now have antibodies in their blood.

African variant made contagious to humans through genetic engineering

The outbreak of MERS-CoV did not receive much attention because there would be no human-to-human contamination. The scientists investigated why not many more Africans - given their many interactions with dromedaries - had not become infected. There, the virus circulates primarily in dromedaries in Morocco, Nigeria, Ethiopia and Burkina Faso. Samples were collected and it turned out that the variants that occur in Arabia can be easily transmitted from person to person, but not those in Africa.

The difference between the variants is in the amino acids of the S protein. By genetically modifying the African variant so that it had the same 'Arabian' amino acids, they succeeded in making the African variant more infectious to human cells as well. The big, unasked question, of course, is: why would you want to do that? Why would you want to make a virus that is (almost) harmless to humans much more infectious, as happened with the coronavirus?

Anyway, the researchers think that the reason that the variants in the Middle East have not yet mutated to infect many people is that the dromedary trade goes almost exclusively one way, from Africa to the Middle East. However, they warn that if that trade reverses at some point, or if another animal also becomes a carrier and is traded to Africa, mutations could occur that could cause a deadly pandemic. (1)

Virus in top 10 WHO

MERS-CoV is very similar to SARS-1 and also causes very severe respiratory symptoms. Among humans, it still has a 35% mortality rate. There is no treatment or vaccine yet. Since 2012, more than 2,100 people have been infected with MERS-CoV, 813 of whom have died. The virus is now in the top 10 of WHO's list of emerging diseases that should be investigated with the highest priority (2).

SPARS = MERS-CoV or SARS-3?

Late last year, the possible successor to Covid-19 was already announced: SPARS. In a simulation by Johns Hopkins University, this pandemic breaks out in 2025, and lasts until 2028.

'The SPARS pandemic 2025 - 2028; A Futuristic Scenario for Public Health Risk Communicators' (PDF, 2017) was a simulation similar to the later 'Event 201' in October 2019, when every detail was practiced on managing a global outbreak with a coronavirus, which, according to the working forecast, would kill 65 million people. That 'simulation', as you all know, became a reality in almost every respect (only the number of deaths, fortunately, remains far behind (yet?)).

In fact, a World Bank document states that the current 'project' called 'Covid-19 Strategic Preparedness and Response Program (SPRP)' will last until March 31, 2025. Only then will SARS-CoV-2 / Covid-19 presumably be declared definitively 'over', although Covid could therefore also be succeeded by MERS-CoV in the meantime.

After that the successor could start to appear immediately: SPARS, which is a reference to the U.S. city of St.Paul where this future coronavirus will first emerge according to the simulation. This new virus will, of course, be renamed in or around 2025, and could also start again in Asia, for example. However, it could also become SARS-3, which is already ready in an Italian laboratory.

So it is not unlikely that SPARS will actually become SARS-3 or MERS-CoV. 2025 was just a fictional year, which could just as easily become 2023 or earlier. The SPARS simulation also talked about a vaccine called COROVAX as the desired solution to stop this "pandemic," and which would be introduced in the scenario in July 2026. Three years after this 2017 document, a COROVAX vaccine was literally being developed.

This is how anti-vaxxers would be convinced

A notable similarity to SARS-CoV-2 / Covid-19 is that the fictional SPARS infection (/ MERS-CoV or SARS-3 infection?) is often followed by severe bacteriological pneumonia (pg. 57). It also describes how a well-known anti-vaxxer "sees the light" after her infant son develops severe pneumonia, and heals only after administration of regular medication. Authorities then use stories like this to convince vaccine opponents.

Striking similarity to 2020-2021: '... several influential politicians and representatives of institutions came under fire for sensationalizing the severity of the event for certain political gain... A broad social media movement, led mainly by outspoken parents of affected children, coupled with the widespread distrust of 'Big Pharma', supported the narrative that the development of SPARS MCMs (vaccines) was unnecessary, and driven by some profit-seeking individuals.'

It also pointed to 'conspiracy theories' that this virus was also intentionally created, and/or deliberately unleashed on the population by the government as a bioweapon (pg. 66). Meanwhile, the 'Fauci Files', published even by American mainstream media, revealed that the coronavirus was internally called a deliberately created bioweapon as early as March 11, 2020.

Unvaccinated will soon be blamed directly

The pharmaceutical manufacturers, who have proven over the past year how extremely profitable vaccinating during a p(l)andemic can be, are busy developing new vaccines. Bloomberg pointed to GlaxoSmithKline (and partner Sanofi) in late May, which is already making the next generation of Covid vaccines. According to Roger Connor, head of vaccine development, a trial period of a new vaccine on more than 37,000 people was to begin as early as June.

Given the increasingly harsh, often shocking reactions in society to people refusing to be vaccinated against Covid-19 (calls for forced vaccinations are getting louder, and the first calls to put refusers in camps have also been heard), we think that we are long past the stage of "convincing" anti-vaxxers, and soon, if this next pandemic does indeed come, will go straight to openly falsely blaming unvaccinated people by politicians and media.

Suppose that vaccines will indeed cause enormous health problems, as top scientists and other experts have been predicting for months (see our many articles on this subject). Then there will be a new run on health care and hospitals, after which harsh measures will again be taken. On TV, 'scientists' approved by the pharma-vaccine complex will claim that it is not because of the vaccines, but because of a mutation that was able to emerge thanks to the unvaccinated people.

Chapter 11: Sars 3

The World Economic Forum, like the World Health Organization, has emerged as one of the most vehement foes of liberty and humanity.

Planned (false flag) WEF cyber attack to destabilize financial system between August 2021 and March 2022 - Will the next "killing virus" be SARS-3, which has already been produced in an Italian laboratory, or SPARS?

The global power elite is so empowered by 90 percent of the population's slavish devotion and naive gullibility that no effort is made to hide the reality that one large planned and predetermined scenario is actually being enacted.

WHO Director Tedros Adhanom Ghebreyesus, a committed communist, is now openly proclaiming the next pandemic, which will be "more more contagious and lethal" than Covid-19, as you may know. Pharmaceutical companies are rubbing their palms together and have already started preparing and testing the next round of vaccinations.

'Make no mistake, this is not the last time the world faces a pandemic threat,' Tedros told the UN General Assembly of 194 member states' health ministers. 'It is an evolutionary certainty that another virus will emerge that is much more contagious and lethal than this one.'

'Evolutionary certainty' was a euphemism for 'this is what we, like Covid-19, have painstakingly developed and planned in collaboration with the World Economic Forum.' Maybe the other virus is SPARS, which we wrote about earlier this year and was supposed to arrive in (about) 2025? Will it be SARS-3, which has already been produced in an Italian facility and might be released on the general public at any time?

'The death toll is dropping, but we're not out of the woods yet.'

Of course, the WHO chief had to declare that the number of Covid-19 cases and deaths had been steadily declining for the past three weeks. To do otherwise would make it very clear that immunizations are having the exact opposite effect in places such as India. Since vaccines began, the number of daily deaths has climbed from 100 to nearly 4500 each day. The guidelines for the heavily overused PCR test were "secretly" modified in January, ostensibly to make the immunizations look successful.

Vaccines are now being evaluated.

Pharmaceutical companies, who have seen how profitable vaccinating during a pandemic can be during the last year, are already working on new vaccinations. Last Monday, Bloomberg reported that GlaxoSmithKline (together with partner Sanofi) is working on the next generation of Covid vaccinations. A trial session using a new vaccination on more than 37,000 patients will begin as early as next week, according to Roger Connor, chief of vaccine development.

It is necessary to bring the population to its knees.

It is now safe to say that the established globalist order, led by the World Economic Forum, the United Nations, the World Health Organization, the International Monetary Fund, the European Union, and the Gavi alliance, and backed by almost every political party, has launched a frontal assault on humanity. As you may be aware, Phase 2 of this pandemic has already been announced: a (false flag) cyber attack on the (bankrupt) Western financial system, as well as possibly the energy supply, with the goal of bringing the population to its knees and forcing them to accept the communist 'Great Reset' ('Build Back Better'), or the 'Fourth Industrial Revolution' in the framework of UN Agenda 21/2030, without resistance.

The WEF has been running simulations, similar to the corona pandemic simulation in October 2019 ('Event 201'), to see how best to carry out such a cyber-attack, which will cut the population off from their bank accounts, possibly the internet, and possibly even (parts of) their energy supply (and thus transportation and food supply) for days-perhaps weeks-and how to make the most of the expected consequences.

According to Armstrong, the recent cyber attack on the Colonial Pipeline in the United States, which was allegedly blocked by hackers and then released after paying a $5 million extortion fee, was also a test to see if the planned cyber attack on the financial system could be carried out in this manner. 'They can now argue that malware is profitable, and the entire globe is at risk.' That's the most likely scenario right now.'

'This threat appears to be motivated by the desire to complete the Great Reset.' Covid was grossly inflated, and those behind the bogus models that were used to flatten the global economy stand to make a lot from inflating this cyber danger. The question now is, when will they do it? 'Will it be this year or next year?'

Chapter 12: Immune system suppression

Covid-19 is "mainly a vascular illness," according to researchers - Circulation Research: Lung injury is aided by spike protein - Your immune system is working against you to protect you from the vaccine.

In a scientific publication, researchers at the famed Salk Institute, which was founded by vaccine pioneer Jonas Salk, indirectly admit that the Covid vaccinations induce life-threatening blood clots and harm to both blood vessels and the immune system.

We noted earlier this week that an increasing number of well-known scientists are coming to the opinion that vaccines are the greatest hazard to human health.

Thousands of Europeans and Americans have already paid with their lives, and hundreds of thousands with their health, for their "voluntary" participation in history's greatest "medical" experiment.

In the West, all Covid vaccinations program the human body to create the spike protein, the most lethal element of the alleged SARS-CoV-2 virus, with the goal of shielding humans against the spike protein's damaging consequences.

In a nutshell, we make your body manufacture something harmful in order for it to generate antibodies against that same danger, but we have no idea how or if this process will ever be stopped.

So why not take the "risk" of getting the virus, which has been shown to not make 99.7% of the population sick, if at all? No, in 2021, that rational, historically uncontroversial line of reasoning is suddenly so antiquated. We can no longer rely on our natural immune system and must instead rely on what is administered through a syringe.

'Covid-19 is mostly a vascular illness,' says the researcher.

The vaccination industry, politicians, and the media continue to insist that the spike protein is safe, but the Salk Institute has now established that this is not the case. On the contrary, the Salk researchers and other scientific colleagues warn in the publication "The spike protein of the new coronavirus plays an extra crucial role in disease" that the spike protein harms cells, "confirming that Covid-19 is largely a vascular illness."

Another spike protein that has claimed so many lives?

Of course, the Salk scientists are forbidden from criticizing vaccines directly. That is why, according to their article, the spike protein produced by vaccines behaves quite differently than the spike protein produced by the alleged virus.

To begin with, this contradicts all vaccine makers' claims that their vaccines create the same spike protein. Second, it casts doubt on the efficacy of vaccines, because if the spike protein produced by vaccines differs significantly from that produced by the virus, what is the point of vaccination (assuming, for the time being, that these genetically designed 'vaccines' operate at all)?

On the plus side, even pro-vaccine scientists now accept that the spike protein is to blame for a large number of deaths and people suffering from major side effects and long-term, often permanent health harm. In other words, it's an implied admission that Covid-19 vaccinations are potentially fatal.

Spike protein causes lung injury, according to research published in Circulation Research.

"The SARS-Cov-2 spike protein impairs endothelial function by inhibiting ACE-2," according to a scientific study published in Circulation Research. The inside of the heart and blood vessels are lined with edothele cells. By decreasing ACE-2 receptors, the spike protein 'promotes lung injury.' The endothelial cells in blood arteries are damaged, and the metabolism is disrupted as a result.

The authors of this study were also pro-vaccination, claiming that "vaccine-generated antibodies" may protect the body from the spike protein. Essentially, the spike protein can cause significant damage to vascular cells, and the immune system can counteract this damage by fighting the spike protein.

The immune system is trying to protect you AGAINST the vaccine

In other words, the human immune system strives to defend the patient from the vaccine's negative effects and counter-reactions in order to prevent the patient from dying. Anyone who survives the Covid vaccine owes it to their own immune system's protection AGAINST the vaccine, not the vaccination itself.

'The vaccination is the weapon,' Mike 'Natural News' Adams concludes. 'Your immune system protects you. All Covid vaccinations should be withdrawn off the market immediately and re-evaluated for long-term negative effects based on this research alone.'

According to official VAERS statistics, the number of vaccine-related deaths in the United States in 2021 will be almost 4000 percent more than the total number of vaccine-related deaths in 2020.

The holy vaccine is not to blame for a heart attack or a cerebral hemorrhage.

The following mechanism has been scientifically proved and is now established: the Covid-19 vaccinations encourage your body to make the spike protein, which can cause vascular damage and blood clots, which can move throughout the body and end up in various organs (heart, lungs, brain, etc.). People who die as a result of this are referred to as having had a "heart attack," "blood clot," or "brain haemorrhage" - the sacrosanct vaccines can and must never be blamed, no matter how much evidence there is today showing they are the main reasons.

Vaccine recipients appear to offer a risk to the unvaccinated, in addition to the possibility for permanent or deadly harm to their own health. Many of the corona'wappies' who have recently had their shots have been transformed into walking'spike factories,' and can now exhale these spike proteins. They can so infect others through this 'shedding' process.

Bioweapon vaccines were created by the apartheid administration against the black population.

Vaccines have long been used as bioweapons against the general public. South Africa's Apartheid Government created the technology underlying such a "self-replicating" vaccination. Scientists were developing 'racial' vaccines at the time, with the goal of eradicating much of the black population.

This year, the Johns Hopkins Bloomberg School of Public Health proposed using a self-replicating vaccine to automatically 'vaccinate' the whole world's population.

Drones and AI robots would subsequently be used to enforce and monitor the program.

People who are still eager to sign up in a vaccine alley to be genetically modified to generate a potentially life-threatening spike protein appear to have been fully misled by the mainstream media and system politicians. They've been numb to all the warnings and the mountains of proof, and they can't believe the world is being ruled by unscrupulous monsters who have no qualms about committing the potentially single biggest genocide in human history.

Chapter 13: Passports & chips

A 2016 interview with WEF senior executive Klaus Schwab, in which he predicts that "within 10 years" an obligatory global health card will be adopted, and everyone will have implanted microchips, adds to the proof that the Covid-19 issue was painstakingly prepared.

Schwab was reportedly working on a plan at least five years ago to create a huge virus outbreak and exploit it to establish health passports and link them to mandatory testing and vaccinations, all according to the problem-reaction-solution approach. The goal is to have complete control over the whole human population on the planet.

'Within 10 years, we will have implanted microchips,' said Schwab five years ago.

In 2016, a French-speaking interviewer asked him, 'Are we talking about implantable chips?' 'When is it going to happen?'

'Absolutely in the next ten years,' said Schwab. 'We'll start by putting them in our clothes.' We can next picture implanting them in our brains or skin.' The WEF foreman then commented on his vision of man and machine 'fusing.'

'In the future, we may be able to communicate directly between our brains and the digital world.' We observe a merger of the physical, digital, and biological worlds.' People will simply have to think about someone in the future to be able to reach them straight through the 'cloud.'

There will be no more biological persons with natural DNA in the transhumanist world, which will finally become fully "digital." The 'cloud' will be used to store everyone's data.

Humanity has begun to be reprogrammed genetically.

The current economic order will be destroyed by Schwab's 'Great Reset' ('Build Back Better'). The looming financial meltdown will be exploited to launch a new global system based only on digital money and transactions. This new system will be connected to the entire world thanks to 5G technology. Refusers will be barred from "buying and selling," in other words, from social life.

In the late 2020s, Covid-19 mRNA 'vaccines' began genetically programming and manipulating humanity in order to make it 'fit' to be first linked, then integrated, with this global digital system, which, as you know, I believe is the Biblical realm of 'the Beast.'

These gene-altering vaccines have the potential to eliminate your free will and ability to think for yourself, as well as your desire and ability to connect with the spiritual realm.

Christian Perspective: Humanity is cut off from God

From a Christian perspective, the reprogramming of human DNA through these vaccines can be seen as Satan's final attempt to permanently separate humankind from God. This appears to be the true explanation for the prophetic Bible book of Revelation's warning that individuals who bear this "mark" will perish.

This isn't simply because of a chip and a succession of pricks; it's because of what those pricks will do to and in you. As a result, God will be unable to save those whose minds (free will) have been reprogrammed to total obedience ('worship'). That will necessitate His intervention, for otherwise, humanity as a whole will be lost forever.

False teachings have blinded a large portion of Christianity.

The essential aspect of this devious plot, which has been in the works for a long time, was the infiltration of Christianity with a series of false teachings, with the goal of keeping believers blind until the end of time in preparation for the advent and establishment of the Beast's rule.

Indeed, tens to hundreds of millions of Christians, particularly in the West, believe that they will never have to live through this period. Even now, when the implementation of this system has begun, the majority of people refuse to accept it. With their pro-vaccination views, most Christian parties and churches are openly cooperating in this "Great Reset" to the domain of "the Beast." In theological terms, the Vatican is the most powerful and convinced driver of this.

'But we were duped!' isn't an excuse.

Perhaps a biblical parallel can help some people understand? Genesis 3, the tale of creation and the 'Fall,' as told to us today: The serpent persuaded Adam and Eve that they were not allowed to 'eat' the 'apple,' in this case the sign, i.e. not to have it pricked in them (root test of 'the sign': charagma = scratch/something with a needle = prick), but the serpent persuaded them that this sign would not damn them, but rather make them into 'gods.' After being persuaded by this falsehood, their complaints against God ('but we've been lied to!') were futile, and they died slowly and painfully. They could have and should have known, thus they had no justification.

Accepting 'the sign,' according to the Bible, carries an even worse consequence: eternal death. Allowing yourself to be genetically modified with mRNA vaccinations and then integrated into a global digital network, so relinquishing all control over your body and free will, will be up to each individual to decide whether the danger is worth it.

Chapter 14: No more freedom

The US federal Occupational Safety and Health Administration (OSHA) is warning employers that they will be held liable for any damage to their employees' health if they are required to be vaccinated against Covid-19. This could become a tricky issue in Europe as well, since the government has rejected all government liability in advance and put it on the plate of health care providers. If in the end no agency wants to take responsibility, then in view of human rights these vaccinations cannot possibly be directly or indirectly made a condition for getting or having a job, or access to buildings and events, as is now the intention.

If a U.S. worker is forced to be injected with these experimental mRNA gene therapies packaged as "vaccines" and is subsequently blinded or paralyzed, or even dies, this injury will be considered "work related," which will make his employer liable. The guidelines also state that employers are required to record (serious) side effects and adverse reactions following Covid vaccinations in their employees.

The new OSHA directive was published on April 20, and was a response to companies and institutions that had announced that all their employees will be required to be vaccinated, such as the Methodist Hospital network in Houston. Those who refuse will first be suspended, and later fired.

Vaccines only have emergency authorization

It is expected that this hospital organization and many other employers will be sued if they follow through with these plans and their employees subsequently become ill or die. According to the VAERS registration system, nearly 200,000 Americans have already suffered health damage from the Covid-19 vaccines, and nearly 4,000 have died. Nearly 20,000 have been seriously (long-term or permanent) injured (autoimmune diseases, paralysis, blindness, the muscle disease ALS, Creutzfeld-Jakob, Alzheimer's, etc.).

America's Frontline Doctors (AFLDS) warns that the vaccines - as in Europe - have only a temporary emergency license, and for that reason alone cannot be imposed on anyone. 'The US Food & Drug Administration's emergency authorization specifically states that individuals should have the free choice to accept or refuse these vaccines,' LifeSiteNews explained. 'Many point out that any dismissal for refusing vaccines absolutely undermines your necessary freedom.'

However, the European Human Rights Court recently ruled that mandatory vaccinations are legal. Still, even in the Netherlands, not one worker should automatically accept that his boss requires a Covid-19 vaccination as a condition for keeping your job, or continuing to do the work for which you were hired.

Chapter 15: No healthcare

Some doctors are so indoctrinated and terrified that they blame the sick themselves: 'My employer put a lot of pressure on me to be vaccinated.'

The Highwire, the fastest growing American Internet health program that already has more than 75 million viewers, recently focused attention on a troubling trend in the U.S. that may also be occurring in other Western countries. In fact, more and more doctors are refusing to treat people who suffer from serious side effects and adverse reactions after vaccination with a Covid-19 vaccine. The reason is obvious: the political and pharmaceutical establishment has effectively canonized these gene-manipulated vaccines. If people do get very sick or even die from them - in the U.S. in 2021 there will already be 4000% more vaccine victims than in the whole of 2020 from all other vaccinations combined - then the instructions are that it cannot and must not be the vaccine's fault. Doctors who nevertheless observe this must fear for their jobs and careers.

Some doctors are so indoctrinated that they blame the sick themselves. They call people who suffer serious side effects after vaccination patients with a 'conversion disorder', afraid to put in their file that the vaccine is the probable cause. (Or, in other words, 'go back home, little lady, because it's between your ears.')

'On January 4, I was put under great pressure by my employer to get vaccinated,' Shawn Skelton told me. After she complied, she immediately experienced side effects such as mild flu-like symptoms. 'But by the end of the day, my legs were hurting so badly that I couldn't take it anymore. When I woke up the next day my tongue was twitching, and then it got worse and worse. The next day I had convulsions all over my body. That lasted 13 days.'

'Too afraid to treat us,' they say.

'One doctor told me the diagnosis was, 'I don't know what's wrong with you, therefore we blame you,'" said another. Skelton elaborated. 'Doctors just do not know how to address the mRNA vaccine's negative effects. I also believe they are terrified of it. I'm at a loss for words as to why no doctor wants to help us.'

Two other healthcare workers, Angelia Desselle and Kristi Simmonds had similar experiences. They too suffered convulsions, and their doctors also refused to treat them. A neurologist rejected Desselle's email referral to him. 'He was a movement disorder specialist, which I thought I needed. My primary care physician said it looked like I had advanced Parkinson's. But he emailed back that he had very complex duties, and he couldn't see me at that time.'

As other doctors likewise kept the door closed to her, she went to a neurologist without mentioning that she

had been vaccinated against Covid-19. 'I didn't want to be sent away again. But it is in my medical record, so when he looked at that he said 'so you took the vaccine?' And I said 'yes, but I didn't want to give you that information because I need help.' Now she is finally receiving treatment for her migraine attacks.
In Europe, general practitioners and specialists are subject to stringent regulations.

We don't know if general practitioners in Europe also refuse to treat vaccinated patients who become unwell. They are, however, prohibited from prescribing proven-effective and safe drugs to (suspected) corona patients, such as hydroxychloroquine and Ivermectin. Nothing should threaten the "holy" mass vaccination program - recovery: genetic engineering program, after all.

In Europe, general practitioners and specialists are subject to stringent regulations.

We don't know if general practitioners in Europe also refuse to treat vaccinated patients who become unwell. They are, however, prohibited from prescribing proven-effective and safe drugs to (suspected) corona patients, such as hydroxychloroquine and Ivermectin. Nothing should threaten the "holy" mass vaccination program - recovery: genetic engineering program, after all.

Earlier this year, the government put any responsibility for the consequences of the Covid vaccinations on the shoulders of health care providers and the people who are vaccinated with them. It is therefore not inconceivable that healthcare professionals and specialists in Europe will be reluctant to recognize, let alone treat, vaccination victims as such.

Chapter 16: Dare to speak

Vaccinating during a pandemic was previously considered "unthinkable" in science - until last year. An investigation has been begun on the growing risks of infection and death among vaccinated people.

Global mass vaccines against Covid-19 are "unthinkable," "unacceptable," and a "historic error," according to Luc Montagnier, a French virologist who won the Nobel Prize in 2008 for discovering HIV. Vaccinations are what cause 'variants,' and individuals die from the sickness as a result of them.

'Isn't this a tremendous oversight? It was both a scientific and a medical error. Montagnier remarked in a translated interview published last Tuesday by the RAIR Foundation USA, "It is an awful mistake." 'This will be documented in history books because the mutations are caused by vaccination.'

Many epidemiologists are aware of this, yet they remain silent about it, even when it comes to well-known issues like 'antibody-dependent enhancement': 'It is the virus's antibodies that allow the illness to worsen,' Montagnier stated earlier this month in an interview with Pierre Barnérias of Hold-Up Media.

Although variants (mutations) do develop naturally (but virtually always become less lethal and thus less hazardous), Covid vaccinations are now the primary drivers of this process. 'What is the virus's function? Is it going to die or will it find another way? The novel variations are clearly formed as a result of the intervention of certain antibodies.'

Vaccinating during pandemics was considered 'unthinkable' in science until last year.

Vaccinating during a pandemic was formerly considered "unthinkable" in science because it has been proven to increase the amount of sick individuals and deaths. Vaccinations have produced and resulted in the new variations. That is something you see in every country; it is the same everywhere. Vaccinations cause mortality in every country.'

Data from the University of Washington's Institute for Health Metrics and Evaluation was used in a video to highlight how the number of deaths rises substantially in all countries where immunizations have been implemented. Montagnier cited official WHO data showing that since the immunizations were started in January, not just the number of deaths, but also the number of new infections and sick persons has increased dramatically, "particularly among young people."

Infections and mortality after vaccines are being studied.

Thrombosis (blood clots) is one of the reasons why numerous countries have ceased using the AstraZeneca vaccine, according to the Nobel winner. He's also working on a study on people who get ill with the coronavirus after getting vaccinated. According to the CDC, at least 5,800 Americans had been affected by the virus by April; 396 of them were hospitalized, and 74 died.

"I will demonstrate that they are developing vaccine-resistant variations." Montagnier made headlines in April 2020 when he said that the SARS-CoV-2 virus had to have been created in a lab. 'The presence of HIV elements and malaria germs in the coronavirus genome is particularly suspicious.' These characteristics of the virus could not have developed spontaneously.' In July 2020, he published a study that backed up his idea.

Is there a mass euthanasia scheme in the works?

The argument that the Covid-19 vaccinations are more akin to a slow-motion euthanasia program, which could result in open genocide on an unprecedented scale in the short to medium term, looks increasingly justified. People who have recently been vaccinated and claim that "nothing bothers them" forget that (severe) vaccination harm might take weeks, months, or even years to manifest.

Because the virus has yet to be isolated anywhere in the globe, some believe the 'new coronavirus' is just a massive scam designed to inject people with this experimental gene therapy. As a result, the foundations are being laid for a transhuman RNA-DNA programming platform that might permanently alter, control, or cripple anyone who has received these vaccines.

Chapter 17: Poison mandate

'Poisoning risk from lethal phosgene gas'

The ingredients of the Moderna Covid-19 'vaccine' have been released by the Connecticut Department of Health. According to the package insert, this vaccine contains 'SM-102,' which is 'not acceptable for human or animal usage,' according to the manufacturer. The producer, Cayman Chemical Company, has told OSHA that this chemical produces 'acute poisoning' and is 'fatal on contact with the skin.' With prolonged or repeated exposure, SM-102 "damages the central nervous system, kidneys, liver, and respiratory system."

In brief, persons who receive this vaccine may become poisoned. Despite this, government and media efforts continue to tout the vaccinations' safety.

The Connecticut Department of Health's complete list of ingredients can be accessed online (archive here) (Natural News mirror Pre-vaccination screening form - V20, and Covid-19 vaccine ingredients list and spike protein schedule).

The government's guidelines to health-care facilities further state that the risk of anaphylactic shock from vaccinations is so high that all vaccination sites should have severe adverse response drugs on hand. Loss of consciousness, disorientation, confusion, weakness, diarrhea, nausea, vomiting, tunnel vision, seeing flashes of light, hearing issues, and hearing loss are among the many reported side effects. (And this for a virus that is completely harmless to 99.7% of the population.)

SM-102

After publishing this information, Hal Turner got numerous emails from people claiming that the SM-102 cautions only apply to chloroform, not Moderna's Covid vaccination. SM-102 is the third most prevalent element on the Moderna 'vaccine' ingredients list, and it IS the component, according to Cayman Chemical Company.'

'Deadly phosgene gas poisoning'

'Chloroform, like any other chemical, degrades. When it comes into contact with oxygen, it decomposes into phosgene gas,' which is a 'very poisonous gas (a mix of carbon monoxide and chlorine) that liquefies at +8 degrees,' according to the Van Dale Large Dictionary. At just 7 parts per million, it is fatal (7 parts per million).

'As a result, everyone who gets this shot could acquire chloroform, which can then decompose into phosgene gas as it circulates through their bodies.' Some, perhaps many, persons may achieve a deadly phosgene gas threshold in their body and die as a result, possibly within 180 days following their second dose.'

Phosgene poisoning can potentially lead to the formation of a pulmonary embolism. The patient's lungs fill with fluid, making it impossible for him or her to breathe - exactly what occurred to serious Covid-19 sufferers last year, placing them in the hospital and requiring life support.

'What an ingenious technique to depopulate the world - no one notices.'

'Once these people crash to the ground like flies, the same folks who gave us the vaccine may easily blame it on a Covid variation,' Turner concluded. 'How tragic that they died as a result of this mutation, which the vaccine failed to protect them from.' Could this be the case of mass murder's 'plausible deniability'? Make your own decision.' (Or it's being used to force yet another vaccine on the public.)

Turner concludes, 'What a fantastic method to depopulate the world.' 'No one notices because the deaths and the prick occur over a long period of time, and the symptoms of phosgene gas are identical to those of Covid.'

Turner's story was quickly labeled as "disinformation" by the Facebook "fact checker" Leadstories.com. Because these kinds of 'fact checkers' have been a major source of disinformation time and time again since last year, and appear to have been set up only to give the mainstream media's false propaganda a 'approval stamp,' this almost automatically means that there may be a large core of truth in it in 2021.

Leaflet with no content

A nurse had previously given Turner images of the
obligatory package insert that will be included in the
Moderna vaccination cartons. 'When I saw this, I was
horrified,' the healthcare professional said. 'Can you tell
me where the ingredients list is?' In fact, it turned out
to be absolutely blank. 'There's nothing I've ever shot
into a patient that looks like that.' They are aware of the
contents.'

When it comes to information leaflets, do you know of a
single vaccinated individual who received or
downloaded and read one prior to 'the jab'? Foodstuffs
must contain a long list of ingredients or they will not be
sold. The same may be said for most common
medicines and consumer goods. So why, of all things, is
there an exception for vaccines? Why is it made as
difficult as possible for you to learn what you're
injecting into your body and the potential
consequences?

Would you buy soup with the label "We'll know if the
ingredients are safe in three years"?

Would vaccination proponents still refuse to consider it
if they read the horrific package insert for the
AstraZeneca/Vaxzevria vaccine, which reads: "Contains
a chimpanzee-derived genetically modified adenovirus
produced in human embryonic kidney cells." GVOs
(genetically modified organisms) are present in this

product.' ('A single dose (0.5 ml) comprises at least 250 million infectious units of chimpanzee adenovirus, which encodes the SARS-CoV-2 spike glycoprotein ChAdOx1-S.')

What about the black-and-white reality that the vaccine's efficacy, stability, and safety do not have to be shown clearly until May 31, 2022? That is not until March 31, 2024, or THREE YEARS from now, for the old and chronically ill (pg.16). What would vaccination supporters do if they went to the grocery to buy a can of soup and saw on the label that it wouldn't be known whether the components in that soup were safe for their health for another year or three? Wouldn't they then decide, "We're not going to do it for a bit, we'll take something else?"

Chapter 18: Toxic blood

For the time being, the Red Cross in Japan and Belgium do not accept blood donations from anyone who have been vaccinated against Covid-19. According to Jeffrey Kingston, head of Asia studies at Temple University, Japan has not forgotten the crisis in the 1980s, when the government approved the use of HIV-infected donor blood. This happened despite the fact that it was already known that heating might kill virus particles in the blood.

Only 2% of Japanese people are still fully vaccinated - recovery: gene manipulation therapy, compared to 35% in the United States. The Japanese government, according to Kingston, is not only bureaucratic, but also cautious. There is a typical waiting period for blood donation after other immunizations. This is 24 hours for influenza, cholera, and tetanus, 2 weeks for hepatitis B, and 4 weeks for measles, mumps, and rubella.

For the time being, the Belgian Red Cross does not accept donations from those who have been vaccinated.

The American Red Cross enables people who have had mRNA corona vaccines to donate blood in the same way that persons who have been infected with the coronavirus are allowed to. We couldn't discover anything concerning blood donations on the Red Cross website, so we think they can continue without limitation.

To date, no respiratory virus has been proved to be transmissible through blood, including coronaviruses and the flu virus. As a result, giving and receiving blood is risk-free,' according to the Belgian Red Cross website.

'However, unlike the usual flu vaccine, you will be momentarily unable to give after having a corona vaccination.' The length of time depends on the brand and whether you have symptoms after receiving the vaccine.' (Italics added) What are the signs and symptoms of? Surely, if you've been vaccinated, you're safe? Aren't these immunizations "proved safe"?

Chapter 19: India is crumbling

Millions of Indians wash in the Ganges River's open sewers, where dozens of bodies are now discovered everyday.

The number of deaths due to Covid-19 each day has risen from less than 100 in January to over 4,500 in May since India began its vaccine campaign. The clear link between immunizations and autism is no longer debatable. Also keep in mind RIVM director Jaap van Dissel's warning from late last year, when he anticipated that immunizations "could initially raise mortality." And that is exactly what is happening in many nations, including India on a massive scale.

Hundreds of dead are discovered in the Ganges every day. Thousands of Indians die every day from illnesses such as tuberculosis, typhoid, malaria, cholera, and influenza as a result of the country's still-poor sanitary and nutritional circumstances.

People who would have received Covid-19 appear to be more susceptible to the once-rare fungal infections mucormycosis and scrub typhus, which prey on the immune system's weakness. Scrub typhus affects about 1 million Asians each year, but the main threat is (drug-resistant) tuberculosis, which affects 2.8 million Indians each year and kills 435,000.

The death toll skyrockets after immunizations begin, going from fewer than 100 per day to over 4500 per day.

Over 186 million Indians have been immunized with the Covid-19 vaccine since January. India was doing quite well before the vaccine campaign began. The average number of deaths linked to Covid increased from well under 100 in the first three months of the global lockdowns to approximately 1000 in September and October 2020, before decreasing back to far under 100 in January.

Then immunizations were implemented, and the death toll skyrocketed to 1500 per day in April and nearly 4500 in May. In fact, 3532 Covid variants are currently circulating in India, all of which appeared nearly immediately after vaccines began.

How is this possible when two-thirds of the population has already developed antibodies, according to a private testing company? In April, the journal Nature asked the same question. Why are 45 times as many people suddenly dying today, if the immunizations were already protecting so many people against Covid-19? Could this be due to Antibody Dependent Enhancement (ADE), which has been warned about by a number of scientists and experts, and which could become a problem in the Netherlands in the fall when the corona and other respiratory viruses return?

'People who have been vaccinated are more susceptible to major illnesses and infections.'

'Not only do vaccines poison people's systems, making them more susceptible to infectious consequences (virus interference), but they also lead the immune system to fail if it is re-exposed to 'live' coronavirus mutations (ADE),' says Mike 'Natural Adams.'

According to Adams, clinical research have indicated that the Covid-19 vaccinations made recipients more vulnerable to more severe illnesses. The large number of patients who have experienced adverse effects from these vaccines, including as tiredness, fever, harvesting problems, lethargy, paralysis, blood clots, and so on, is proof that they induce significant illnesses, further weakening the immune system.

'Bioweapons of autoimmunity'

'A widespread vaccination program could encourage coronaviruses to evolve even quicker, resulting in increased Spike protein change and, as a result, the creation of novel varieties. The B.1.617.2 variety spreading in India, according to British scientists, is 50 percent more contagious.' By the way, this is a common occurrence; changing viruses always get more contagious, but almost usually become less lethal. However, thanks to vaccines, this time could be different, as the bloodbath in India seem to imply.

Furthermore, these vaccinations act as autoimmune disease bioweapons, prompting people's bodies to manufacture Spike proteins, which can be released into the environment and lead to the rapid evolution of infectious virus particles. After that, the unvaccinated are exposed to a variety of Spike proteins from the vaccinated. This could explain why India's death toll has suddenly skyrocketed, and why bodies are washing up in droves along the Ganges' banks.'

Chapter 20: Total control?

The first components required to transform the entire human race into total techno-slaves are already being extensively distributed.

Radio waves and magnetic fields can be used to make brain and nerve cells sensitive - controlling human behavior in locations with particular radiation is becoming a reality.

Researchers in the United States have created a magnetic protein that can be used to stimulate brain cells quickly (and vice versa). This novel technique can be used to regulate the areas of the brain responsible for complicated behavior.

Because the development of the Spike protein is important to mRNA vaccinations against the coronavirus, it's easy to envisage that in the future, this sort of vaccine will include another "program" that develops a protein meant to obtain external control over our behavior and thoughts.

Optogenetics is being phased out in favor of chemogenetics.

Optogenetics is the most powerful approach. Laser light pulses can be used to switch on or off clusters of associated neurons. Chemogenetics is a new approach that has recently been created. This works by activating customized proteins with "designer pharmaceuticals" (drugs, vaccinations) that can be targeted to certain cell types.

The downside of optogenetics is that it necessitates the introduction of fiber optic wires into the brain, which can only penetrate the tissue to a limited amount. Chemogenetics uses biological reactions to activate nerve cells in a matter of seconds. It is no longer necessary to "open up" the brain with this new approach.

Project magneto

Previous research has shown that nerve cells' heat and mechanical pressure-activated proteins can be genetically changed to become responsive to radio waves and magnetic fields. Attaching a (para)magnetic particle to them, as well as short DNA sequences, accomplishes this. This method has already been utilized to control glucose levels in mice's blood.

In a lab experiment, the created 'Magneto' protein was found to be capable of being taken up by human kidney cells. The protein was then triggered using a magnetic field. 'Magneto' was then put into the genome of a virus, together with a green fluorescent protein and DNA sequences that exclusively target specific types of neurons, in a subsequent test. After that, the virus was delivered into the brains of mice. Magneto was activated there using a magnetic field, causing the (brain) cells to create particular nerve impulses.

Then it was the turn of the mice who could move about freely. Magneto was injected into the region of the brain that controls motivation and reward (dopamine neurons). The mice were then separated into groups and placed in a room where some were exposed to a magnetic field while others were not.

The Magneto mice were found to spend significantly more time in the magnetic area because dopamine neurons in their brains were engaged, giving them a sense of reward when they were there. This demonstrated that complicated behavior may be controlled and even directed by employing Magneto neurons located deep in the brain.

Steve Ramirez, a Harvard neurologist, is ecstatic about the new strategy. 'This method consists of a single, beautiful virus that can be injected anywhere in the brain,' says the researcher. To alter the behavior of the animals (and later humans?), they merely needed to be exposed to a magnetic field.

Controlling your behavior in a radiation-affected area is becoming more feasible.

Now that humans in the year 2021 are having genetic (mRNA) instructions injected into their systems under the pretext of "vaccines" to produce a protein (the

Spike protein), the next step is to add OTHER instructions to these types of vaccines. In a 2017 speech, Moderna's CMO outlined how mRNA can be used to edit people's DNA, making mRNA "vaccines" a platform via which humans can be programmed.

And it appears that this is exactly what will be done, with proteins that will change your behavior when you are in an area with certain radiation coming soon (such as 5G). Until it is a fait accompli, the mainstream media will no certainly call it a "conspiracy theory" or "disinformation." Protesting then becomes meaningless, as you will most likely not be able or willing to do so due to this new technology.

As a result, when WEF CEO Klaus Schwab declared last year that you will "own nothing and be happy" by 2030 (but maybe much sooner), he was dead serious. You will, in fact, be hardwired to be happy no matter what the circumstances are. Some people appear to be impatient to surrender their humanity, independent thought, and even their "soul" in order to become willless, programmed, controlled, and digitally managed system slaves.

Chapter 21: Mask the sheep

Scientists believe that face masks worn by the general public pose an infection risk - For over a century, all pandemic experiences have demonstrated that face masks do not work in fighting viruses and are ineffective as protection.

Recently, the mainstream media triumphantly released a study proving that face masks are effective. However, a brief look at the study's commissioner revealed all: the Max Planck Institute, which is substantially supported by the German government and the European Union. What is today considered 'science' will almost certainly be 'whose bread you eat...' in 2020 and 2021.

As a result, we can no longer anticipate impartial or critical conclusions from these types of 'we of WC duck...' researchers; instead, they let themselves to be exploited, just as they were in the past, to stamp government programs with approbation. In fact, a recent comprehensive German meta-study concluded that face masks are not only ineffective but also hazardous to one's health.

After an hour of reading on the Max Planck Institute's website, it's evident that the institutes and scientists linked with them are like two hands in one glove when it comes to dealing with the government. There are no critical notes, and there isn't a single study that contradicts the authorities' claims even marginally. We also read a request to do more to combat anti-vaccine voices, such as banning them from the Internet, in order to make it more "democratic"...

The Inquisition has returned under another name

The politically powerful Catholic Church dragged Galileo Galilei before the Inquisition at the beginning of the 17th century because, like Copernicus in the 16th century, he claimed that the earth, like the other planets, revolves around the sun (the heliocentric worldview), and that we are not the center of the universe (the geocentric worldview). To 'prove' him wrong, several established'scientists' and'scientific' and theological theses were quoted. Only in 1992 did the then-Pope John Paul II apologize, and the Vatican cleansed his name.

Face masks are ineffective and (very) hazardous to one's health, according to a metastudy.

However, there are still those scientists who have not sold their souls to the devil. For example, a recent German meta-study confirmed what has been known for over a century: face masks are ineffective and harmful to one's health. Twenty-two of the 44 scientific research that found substantial detrimental effects of face masks were published in 2020, and twenty-two of those studies were published under Covid-19. There were 31 experimental studies and 13 observational studies in total. The well-known blue face masks and N95 mouthmasks drew 68 percent of the attention.

Exhaustion, confusion, and sickness are caused by increased respiratory difficulty, heart rate, and blood pressure.

Wearing surgical (blue) mouth caps by healthy healthcare workers (18 to 40 years old) causes measurable physical effects with increased transcutaneous (through the skin) CO2 values and significant changes in blood composition after only 30 minutes, according to a randomized crossover study published in 2005. The considerable rise in CO2 "breathing back in" causes increased respiratory resistance, requiring the body to exert increasing amounts of effort, as well as a large increase in heart rate.

The negative effects may appear minor at first, but wearing face masks on a regular basis adds up to an increasing physical load. Face masks are predicted to have disease-relevant impacts in the long run, according to the warning. High blood pressure, arteriosclerosis, heart disease (metabolic syndrome), and neurological diseases are just a few of the unavoidable side effects of long-term use of mouth masks.

Even a small increase in CO2 in the inhaled air causes headaches, respiratory issues (asthma), elevated blood pressure and heart rate, which causes blood vessel

111

damage, and finally neuropathological and cardiovascular disorders. Only slightly raised respiratory pressure over a long period of time has similar effect. Elevated CO2 levels are especially dangerous for pregnant women because they impair the placenta's blood supply.

Panic attacks, hyperventilation, cognitive difficulties, and headaches are all symptoms of stress.

It has been established beyond a reasonable doubt that face masks cause significant and, in the long run, lasting health damage. The stress hormone norepinephrine is released very instantly by the human brain in response to low oxygen levels and slightly increased CO2 consumption. The CO2 level only needs to be 5% to produce a panic attack in 15 to 16 minutes, according to breath provocation experiments. The usual CO2 concentration in exhaled air is around 4%.

Mouth caps are contraindicated for epileptics, according to neurologists from the United States, the United Kingdom, and Israel, since they can cause hyperventilation. In fact, wearing a face mask can raise your breathing rate by 15% to 20%.

The use of mouthpieces caused 71.4 percent of 343 health care employees in New York to experience recognized physical (illness) symptoms. Even worse, 28% had chronic health issues for which they needed medication.

Within the context of Covid-19, all varieties of face masks were evaluated in depth in 2020. Conclusion: After only 100 minutes, they create severe thinking and concentration issues, which are produced directly by the decreasing oxygen content in the blood. Another study discovered that face masks are directly responsible for more than half of the headaches experienced by face mask users.

Infections and skin conditions

Because mouth caps cover the respiratory tract, body temperature rises and humidity rises, drastically altering the skin's natural habitat. Many people have red, itchy, and dry skin, as well as excessive sebum production (acne). It worsens and prolongs skin disorders, making people more susceptible to infections. This is because both the blue and N95 face masks allow germs, fungus, and viruses to multiply fast both within and outside the face masks (which are saturated after only 10-15 minutes and then no longer operate anyhow).

The skin on your face is not meant to stay hidden for long periods of time. Large numbers of people will experience undesirable skin problems now that it is required to do so anyway.

Significant psychological harm, particularly among children

Psychological damage has been documented in addition to the numerous physical repercussions and substantially diminished quality of life - because even regular daily activities such as eating, drinking, and conversing are badly affected. Face masks cause a sensation of loss of freedom and autonomy (which may very well be the aim of the wearing requirement), which can lead to suppressed rage and unconscious continual distraction, especially since face masks are frequently imposed by others.

Face masks jeopardize basic human rights such as personal integrity, the right to self-determination, and autonomy, in addition to causing discomfort and resulting in the loss of certain psychomotor, cognitive, and mental abilities, as well as reduced reactivity. Face masks are especially damaging to children, who often experience worry and tension as a result of them. Many youngsters get unwell and unhappy, retreat, and engage less in life. (An entire generation of youngsters and teenagers has thus been severely harmed.)

The media, both now and in the past, has played a very harmful role.

Depressive feelings are widespread, with 50 percent of the oral health wearers polled experiencing them. The concern is exacerbated by the mainstream media's frequently exaggerated and one-sided reporting. Only 38% of media coverage of the Ebola pandemic in 2014 contained scientific fact, and 42% (significantly) overstated the danger, according to a research. A shocking 72 percent of media pieces were designed to make viewers feel worse about their health.

We don't have hard numbers yet, but we believe that by 2020, just 10% of news coverage will contain any scientific fact, and 90% will (seriously) hype the coronavirus's danger. And, with a few exceptions, all mainstream media were and are guilty of instilling feelings of fear and uncertainty 24 hours a day, 7 days a week.

Face masks are a symbol of pseudo-solidarity and conformity.'

According to scientists in one of the papers analyzed, face masks have become "a symbol of conformity and pseudo-solidarity." The WHO, for example, exclusively emphasizes the ostensible 'benefits' of wearing face masks and attempts to create in the wearers the (false) belief that they are helping to combat a virus.

Meta-study conclusion: 'The potentially drastic and undesirable effects observed in multidisciplinary fields underscore the general scope of global decisions to introduce face masks... According to the literature, there are unequivocal, scientifically substantiated undesirable consequences for face mask wearers, both physical, psychological and social.'

'There is no scientific evidence that the virus has been eradicated.'

'Neither the WHO, the ECDC (European Centre for Disease Prevention and Control), nor national institutes (such as the RIVM) have proven with well-founded scientific data a positive consequence of face masks for the population (in the sense of a reduced spread of Covid-19),' the harsh face mask judgment reads.

'National and international health authorities have imposed their theoretical judgements on face masks on society, contrary to the scientifically established standard of evidence-based medicine, even though the mandatory wearing of face masks creates a deceptive sense of security.'

'Face masks worn by the general public pose a risk of infection.'

'From an infectious epidemiology standpoint, regular usage of face masks exposes wearers to the danger of self-contamination from both the inside and outside (of the face masks), as well as through contaminated hands. Furthermore, exhaled air causes face masks to get saturated, allowing infection-causing chemicals to gather on the inside. This tendency may be evidenced by the remarkable surge in rhinoviruses in the RKI (German National Institute of Public Health and the Environment) Sentinel research starting in 2020.'

116

'Face masks worn by the public are considered an infection risk by scientists, since standardized hygiene rules in hospitals cannot be followed by society.' On top of that, the forced 'having to speak louder under a face mask leads to an increased production of aerosols (the atomization effect)' (which can be measured up to 20 meters away, and which automatically makes all the social distancing completely useless, since face masks are thus saturated after only 10 - 15 minutes and no longer work anyway. And who replaces his or her face mask every 10 minutes?).

Face masks do not aid in any modern epidemic.

Face masks in daily usage failed to accomplish the hoped-for results in the fight against viral infections during the influenza pandemics of 1918-1919, 1957-1958, 1968, 2002, and with SARS 2004-2005, as well as the influenza of 2009 (swine flu).

The experiences prompted scientific studies, which concluded in 2009 that daily usage of face masks has no substantial antiviral effect. Even later, scientists and institutes determined that the face masks were ineffective in protecting users from viral respiratory infections. Surgical face masks, even when used in hospitals, lack solid evidence of virus prevention.'

'As always, no favorable benefits on infections or diseases have been detected in a practical comparison between Sweden and Belarus on the one hand and the rest of Europe, as well as the United States (between the states with and without mandatory face masks).

Chapter 22: Vaccine victims

'Thousands of avoidable deaths due to Covid, and thousands already owing to vaccines' - India halts death explosion following Ivermectin and hydroxychloroquine vaccinations - Could it be the same here with the same immunizations if such procedures are used in America?

Professor Dr. Peter McCullough, one of the world's foremost authorities on the treatment of Covid-19, accused the US government of concealing "unimaginable numbers" of vaccine victims in an interview.

This is exactly the scenario we've been forecasting for almost a year: vaccines produce enormous numbers of new casualties, which are then attributed to a Covid variation or some other cause of death, as is most likely the case in, example, India. Could this be the case here as well, if such techniques are already being used in America to persuade as many people as possible to take these 'vaccines'?

We are now being controlled by the same power elite (WEF, UN/WHO, Gavi/Gates, Big Pharma).

With the VAERS vaccination registration system in the United States, the number of reported vaccination deaths is approaching 5000, up from roughly 1% to a maximum of 10% of the real number in the past. As of May 15, about 11,500 individuals have been injured in the EU, with over 630,000 individuals hurt on both sides of the Atlantic and tens of thousands more people permanently ill or incapacitated. Because the number of vaccine victims is thousands of times larger than all other vaccines combined, a detailed study is usually required.

A medication is normally taken off the market after 50 deaths.

'Any new drug with five unexplained deaths gets a 'black box' warning, and then you hear on the news that this drug can kill you,' McCullough explained. 'And after 50 deaths, it's removed off the market,' says the author.

During the 1976 swine flu pandemic, the US sought to vaccinate 55 million people, but the effort was halted after 25 people died and 500 people were crippled as a result of the vaccine.

Now the exact opposite is happening in both America and Europe: the further the number of victims rises, the more pressure the authorities exert on the population to be vaccinated. And all this with substances that have only been provisionally approved, and whose producers will only have to prove that they are 'safe' in a few years' time.

'It would be impossible for civil service doctors to certify that deaths were not caused by immunizations in such a short period of time.'

The numbers are even falsified on purpose, according to the esteemed academic. At the end of March, there had been 2,602 vaccine-related deaths in the United States. The FDA then said that 1600 deaths had been 'investigated' by anonymous government doctors, who had come to the conclusion that none of these persons had died as a result of the vaccine.

'That was disturbing,' McCullough said. He knows from his own experience that it normally takes months to complete such an investigation, not just a few days or weeks. 'I've been chairman and participated on dozens of safety monitoring boards ... and I can tell you that there is no way that unknown civil service doctors without any experience with Covid-19 can determine that not one of these deaths was due to the vaccine.'

Many more people are dying in actuality.

Because only 1% to 10% of vaccine deaths are reported historically, as validated by a Harvard study, many more people will die in actuality than are reported in official estimates, and certainly not 0.
Because only 1% to 10% of vaccine deaths are reported historically, as validated by a Harvard study, many more people will die in actuality than are reported in official estimates, and certainly not 0.

Compare it to the flu vaccination. Annually, the VAERS reports 20-30 deaths, out of 195 million vaccinations.

121

With Covid-19, the US was already at 2602 deaths at 77 million vaccinations, by far the highest number for vaccines in all of history. Despite this, not one established politician or journalist in the mass media is demanding an independent investigation. Worse, the few who do are immediately stigmatized and reviled.

'It is estimated that 85 percent of all lives lost could have been saved.'

The Covid expert thinks that the thousands of deaths (about 16000 in the EU and the US in mid-May, certainly at least 1000 to 2000 more by now) and hundreds of thousands of sick and wounded will continue indefinitely. Furthermore, he said before the United States Senate on November 19, 2020, that "we now believe that up to 85% of the lives lost may have been saved with a multi-drug regimen."

However, those proven working and safe drugs are strictly prohibited in America, Europe and the Netherlands to apply to (presumed) Covid-19 patients. general practitioners can be fined €150,000 if they prescribe Ivermectin.

The government is completely in the bag of Big Pharma and Bill Gates-controlled institutions such as the WHO, and has decided from the outset that only a vaccine may bring 'salvation'.

India uses Ivermectin and HCQ to put a stop to the mortality toll.

India has begun employing Ivermectin and hydroxychloroquine, much against the interests of the WHO and Big Pharma (HCQ). As a result, the enormous increase in the number of deaths following the introduction of vaccinations has now come to an end.

The mainstream media has been told not to publish any criticism of vaccines.

All mainstream media, on the other hand, has been told to portray these drugs in a negative light and to publish (almost) no critical reporting concerning vaccines. They even purposefully generate as much anxiety as possible in Europe at the government's request.

This blatant censorship and total media corruption falls under the Trusted News Initiative, in which not only the social media giants such as Facebook, Google/YouTube and Twitter but also the major news agencies AP, Reuters and AFP participate, as well as the BBC, CBC, EBU (European Broadcasting Union), Microsoft and the Washington Post. Facts about the dark side of experimental gene-therapy vaccinations should be called "dangerous disinformation" by the mainstream media.

Since it results in so many avoidable deaths, how can this be labeled anything other than medical fascism or even medical terrorism?

'If citizens were given 'any type of honest, balanced news on safety,' McCullough concluded, 'they simply would not take this vaccine.' 'The Trusted News Initiative is really concerning, because we are currently experiencing a record number of deaths, which is increasing daily.'

The government and Big Pharma have a symbiotic connection.

The renowned physician claimed that the government and Big Pharma have an incestuous relationship, which prohibits regulatory organizations such as the WHO from being able, willing, or able to deliver an objective judgement. The American National Institutes of Health, for example, is a co-owner of the Moderna patent. As a result, the government has a financial incentive to sell and administer as many vaccines as feasible.

The few doctors, scientists and other professionals who do listen to their conscience are usually too afraid to speak out by name. Understandably, because otherwise since last year it is not only immediately the end of license or end of career, but you are also dragged through the mud and in some cases even sued and / or intimidated by the same government.

'We never find out the true number of casualties.'

According to a recent assessment of 500 nursing home residents conducted by a Kansas City doctor, 22 elderly persons died within 48 hours of receiving a Pfizer shot. 'I can't prove that the vaccine killed them all, but I can show that it killed them all within 48 hours. They only have to be monitored for 15 minutes, according to the guidelines, so we never get to see the real numbers. It's tough to prove if it happens after those 15 minutes... May God help us if the FDA authorizes this.

One courageous Canadian physician did step into the open. Dr. Charles Hoffe broke with a government ban on him speaking, saying that 'the Moderna vaccine has killed and disabled patients.'

'The government has never been interested in treating sick people.'

According to McCullough, the government had little interest in treating sick people (with drugs), but instead quickly adopted the WHO agenda (social distancing only, face masks, lockdowns, testing, and waiting for vaccinations).

He describes a four-step strategy in his paper "A Guide for Home-Based Covid-19 Treatment: A Step-by-Step Doctor's Plan That Could Save Your Life" (December 2020), where the most important pillar, treating and curing Covid-19 patients with proven and safe medications, has been completely absent from public policy. He believes that as a result, tens of thousands of people have died needlessly in the United States alone.

Last year, French academic Christian Perronne, who has a long and illustrious career, wrote a book with the provocative title "Is There a Mistake They Didn't Make?" - Covid-19: The holy marriage of incompetence and hubris.' According to him, if corona patients had been treated with zinc, hydroxychloroquine/quercetin, vitamins C and D, and azithromycin from the start (especially as a preventive measure), there would have been few deaths and 25,000 French people (80 percent of the death toll at the time) would still be alive today.

Chapter 23: Humanity is shrinking

Earth is still incredibly barren: there are few indications of human civilization visible from space. - 'In New York, all of the people on the planet will fit into one-story buildings.' - "Having children should actually be a societal duty," says a Tesla executive who is focused on human RNA and DNA programming.

Elon Musk, the CEO of Tesla, is notorious for making statements that contradict the globalist 'New World Order' image. In a recent address, he stated that our greatest challenge in 20 years will be underpopulation, not overpopulation. We previously said that, contrary to common assumption, the Earth has more than enough room, food, energy, and riches to support at least three times as many people in a prosperous existence. As soon as possible. The true source of our greatest concern is the global power elite, who are doing everything imaginable to eliminate as many people as possible by keeping them impoverished, sick, hungry, and therefore controllable.

'I want to emphasize that the biggest issue in 20 years is population collapse, not an explosion.' He gives as a simple example someone who randomly drops a bomb from an airplane somewhere on earth. 'How often do you hit someone then? As a matter of fact, never. All kinds of stuff falls to Earth from space all the time. Natural meteorites, old rocket parts, but nobody worries about that.'

'Having children should almost be regarded as a social obligation.'

'All of the people in the planet could fit on one floor in New York.' The other floors are unnecessary.' According to Musk, we are so thinly dispersed throughout the world that we are barely visible from space. 'We must be wary about population collapse.' A low birth rate is a major danger.' He cautions that as a result, our culture may perish. 'That would be a depressing conclusion.' The average age would be extremely high, and the young would be forced to care for the elderly like slaves.'

'I believe that, to some extent, people must begin to regard having children as a civic obligation... Otherwise, humanity will perish. Quite literally. Wealth, education, and religion are all inversely connected to the birth rate. The more devout a person is, the more children he or she has.' It will be "as if someone killed half the (future) population" in a few decades. Something needs to be turned around.'

'As quickly as feasible, we must abandon fossil fuels'

Musk is, of course, totally committed to the green'sustainability' mission as an e-car creator and producer. He is upbeat about this since he feels China is also leading the way in this area, having already produced half of the world's electric vehicles. He believes that the world should transition away from fossil fuels as soon as feasible and toward "sustainable" solar, wind, and water energy, as well as nuclear energy in some situations.

The Tesla front man says that oil, gas and coal are running out fast, but forgets that this has been shouted for almost 50 years, and new reserves are constantly being discovered that can provide humanity with cheap energy for at least another century, and probably even many centuries.

Why are there CO2 taxes?

He also contends that society is not being charged for the full price of fossil fuels and CO2 emissions. As a result, he advocates for hefty global CO2 taxes.

Here too he forgets something important, namely that on a geological time scale there is still extremely little CO2 in the atmosphere (about 450 ppm), and that despite all human CO2 emissions (which is only a percentage of far behind the decimal point). Moreover, all the geological evidence shows that CO2 levels only rise after temperatures rise, and not the other way around, as has been claimed for so long. This lie is maintained in order to get the population to agree to ever higher taxes and to cut off their cheap energy supply.

Even if the energy needs of humanity would stop increasing, our planet does not have enough land surface to build enough windmills and solar parks. Not to mention the gigantic load of steel and rare metals that would be needed, plus the fact that especially windmills have an extremely short lifespan (max. 20 years, practice shows that the first mills fail after just a few years. Cleaning up broken windmills is also a very costly affair).

Synthetic RNA and DNA are used to program people.

Musk is also a strong supporter of programmable (synthetic) RNA and DNA, which the Covid-19 vaccinations have already injected into a huge portion of the world's population. 'That reminds me of a computer program.' If you want to, you can probably stop and reverse the aging process with it.'

We have shown that the real goals of creating 'programmable' humans are much more sinister, and seem to be primarily aimed at totalitarian population and behavioral control, and massive population reduction.

Nevertheless, it is nice to hear for once a well-known top executive who has a positive view of humanity, something that can certainly not be said of the globalist climate-vaccine sect led by Klaus Schwab and Bill Gates.

Our other books

Check out our other books for other unreported news, exposed facts and debunked truths, and more.

Join the exclusive Rebel Press Media Circle!

You will get new updates about the unreported reality delivered in your inbox every Friday.

Sign up here today:

https://campsite.bio/rebelpressmedia